YOU ARE PSYCHIC

The Incredible Story of DAVID N. BUBAR

YOU

ARE

PSYCHIC

The Incredible Story of DAVID N. BUBAR

By RENE NOORBERGEN

 William Morrow and Company, Inc.

NEW YORK

Fondly dedicated to
the three girls
in my life:
Dawn
Wendy
and Judie—my wife

PROLOGUE

"Have you ever heard of David Bubar?"

It was Paul Ott Carruth, a young Mississippi television producer and close friend of Jeane Dixon's who shot this question at me while we were driving back to the White House Motor Inn in Baton Rouge, Louisiana. We had spent a few days there in connection with some promotional activities dealing with the book, *Jeane Dixon—My Life and Prophecies*, of which I was the co-author, and had been exchanging pointed views on various well-known American psychics and their sometimes debatable claims to fame.

Paul was acquainted with many of these psychics, and I sensed a deeper meaning behind his casual question.

I glanced at him.

"No, who is he?"

Paul depressed the brake pedal and brought the car to a deliberate stop. Gazing out over the moonlit pond separating the motel from the governor's mansion, his eyes traced the glimmering reflection of the gas lanterns at the water's edge.

He was silent a moment before letting go of the wheel and turning to me.

"Let me tell you about him," he said softly. And as if composing the introduction to a television play, he carefully proceeded to set the stage for the story of David, the forty-two-year-old psychic, a Baptist minister, son of a minister-legislator. The more he talked, the more fascinated and engrossed I became in David's life. It dawned on me that if Paul was correct, he might very well have put me on the trail of one of America's most exciting psychics. The story seemed so incredible, so unbelievable, that it ofttimes crossed the hazy dividing line between reality and science-fiction, leaving me in the tight grasp of that unknown realm of what has often been referred to as the sixth dimension.

Some months later, I began to investigate the tale of David. David Noble Bubar is real—have no doubt about that!

There is a man alive today who will proudly tell you the story of how Bubar pointed to a map of the rugged terrain of British Columbia, marking the exact spot where miners would find a fantastically rich silver vein—a vein that was found shortly thereafter, bringing new prosperity to that part of western Canada.

Others will reluctantly take you in their confidence and share with you the moment when, in the midst of a conversation, David burst out crying, overwhelmed by a sudden, almost devastating sadness.

When asked about the reason for his grief, David choked. "I see a dear friend of mine approach his death. It will happen within the next fifteen minutes, but I am powerless to do anything about it."

His psychic sense is always with him, and when standing one day before a freshly dug grave he told police the identity of the killer of the man they had just buried. It startled neither him nor his friends, for this is the life of David Bubar.

There is this and much more, for David's reputation as a clairvoyant did not come overnight. It began at an early age and manifested itself in hundreds of psychic happenings that brought his P.A.Q. (Prediction Accuracy Quotient) to the ninety percent mark.

I became fascinated with the Bubar story right from the beginning and set out to prove or discredit his claims with or without his cooperation.

Are psychics born? Are they *made?*

The ancient seer Nostradamus was convinced that the psychic had a gift of the gods granted only to those who walked in their presence. Nationally known psychic Helen Stalls, who predicted the death of President Kennedy, is said to have remarked to friends that the real psychics are those who are born with the "gift." Jeane Dixon, another American seer, tends to agree with her, for she too claims to have been born with it, and is convinced that it cannot be taught to anyone. Peter Hurkos, the Dutch clairvoyant, was an ordinary house painter until his near-fatal fall from a ladder. From that moment his entire life changed, and he saw the future around him as an open book.

Recently an ever-increasing number of pseudopsychics have entered this lucrative field, predicting major world events according to what they claim is information received from "above," while actually quoting verses from the works of Nostradamus, the sixteenth-century French psychic, or rewording the predictions of America's Edgar Cayce.

If the opinions of renowned experts in the field of psychic research have any value, then one tends to believe that borrowing predictions from the old masters is an accepted trick of the trade.

Andreja Puharich, brilliant research scientist of the Round Table Laboratories at Glen Cove, Long Island, is convinced that our destinies are very much in the hands of the Eternal

Powers. He holds that because of this, our ability to change this pattern is limited. Everything in this universe, according to Puharich, follows a predestined, inflexible set of rules, and inasmuch as we are part of this creation, this inflexibility also applies to us and forces us to act and react according to these laws.

"This," he claims, "is why psychics and sensitives can look into the future, for it is already there, waiting for us."

Whether or not this is true, most psychic practitioners will readily agree that being a psychic or a clairvoyant is not as unusual as often thought. Supercomedian Jackie Gleason has been interested in the psychic world or the depths of the sixth dimension ever since his thirteenth birthday. *Strange Prophecies That Came True*, by Steward Robb, credits Gleason with having a psychic library of over four thousand books, and quotes Gleason's conclusion after having studied all available material on psychic phenomena:

"Man will again achieve the ability he once possessed in his primitive stage before he developed speech: the ability to communicate normally through Extra-Sensory Perception."

Other researchers back him in this view.

One of the world's most knowledgeable experts, Dr. F. Regis Reisenman, has tested thousands of people before and after he became interested in Jeane Dixon in 1959, and has come to the conclusion that everyone is psychic, often without realizing it. He too is convinced that the psychic sense was much more developed in primitive times, when man had to fight for his existence.

"If man had not been able to sense danger around the corner," he stresses, "he would never have been able to survive in this hostile world." And of course, we wouldn't be here today to talk about it.

In his book *The Reluctant Prophet*, seer David Logan bears out this feeling.

"I am convinced that everyone is psychic to a certain degree," says the man who has often been called thought-provoking. "Though the degree may differ from person to person just like any other talent. Everyone for example has the physical apparatus necessary for seeing. Some people see extremely well, but others almost not at all."

There is little doubt that the inborn psychic ability of man must be on a higher and more sophisticated level than that of the lower animals. Yet for some mysterious reason, they seem to be ahead of us. When we hear a dog howl in agony at the precise moment his master dies miles and miles away, witness flocks of birds take to flight from an area of impending danger, see the agitation and unrest of animals prior to a devastating storm or see fish battle their way across oceans and up treacherous rapids in order to spawn where their ancestors did, we accept these phenomena as absolutely normal. But these are in reality examples of psychic phenomena! In spiritualistic seances, it is often an animal that recognizes the presence of an unknown entity long before the medium does. The animal invariably reveals this awareness through a display of extreme fright or anger. They see, yet they are "lower" animals. Are our minds perhaps dulled through neglect of our psychic faculties? Are we perhaps supposed to "see," yet don't?

Psychics who are sensitive to these phenomena can be divided into various classes, depending on their ability to penetrate the unknown. The most memorable messages given to some of the greatest clairvoyants have come, it is claimed, to them through "angelic messengers."

A vision dealing directly with the future of the United States came to George Washington during one of the bleakest points of this country's history.

During the winter of 1777, while resting at Valley Forge, during the darkest point of the Revolutionary War, Washington was sitting quietly behind his desk in the field command tent working at a dispatch when suddenly a mysterious being materialized at his side, silently observing him at work.

Finally replying to Washington's repeated demands for an explanation about its presence in his tent, the being stated: "Son of the Republic—look and learn!" And while he watched in amazement, a gigantic map of the world appeared through a dense mist, and in slow succession the being showed him the outcome of the Revolutionary War, the beginning and end of the Civil War, and another, totally devastating, war with foreign troops fighting on American soil.

After revealing these tragedies to Washington and forcing him to listen to the bloodcurdling screams of the inhabitants and witness the massacres and total destruction of the country, the visitor said, "Son of the Republic—what you have just seen is thus interpreted. Three great perils will come upon the Republic; the most fearful is the third passing, which the whole world united shall not prevail against.

"Let every child of the Republic learn to live for his God, his Land, and his Union."

And while George Washington's mind was still tortured with this prophetic vision, the being vanished.

Having grown up with awareness of psychic phenomena, David Bubar looks upon these visions and visitations as normal and well within reach of all.

"Clairvoyance and so-called extrasensory perception," he believes, "are not things that have been reserved for the very few. They belong to everyone. Either you are born with a well-developed psychic sense, or you learn to extend the reach of the inherent psychic ability. It's yours for the asking. Every one is psychic—there is no exception!"

Backed by this conviction, he has "turned on" this latent gift within many of his followers and, in this book, presents his method so that each of us can develop his own psychic sense. Little wonder he has gained a tremendous reputation as one of the greatest psychics of today. Glowing adjectives are often used to express the impact of a person's convictions upon those around him; with Bubar, cold statistics would be more telling, for those that apply to him are truly impressive.

Ever since he left the formal ministry—a pulpit in a Baptist church in Stanton, Tennessee, where he preached for seven years—he has given himself completely to psychic counseling and has created a tremendous following. Aided by a staff of two full-time secretaries, six practically full-time volunteers and an impressive array of office machinery including modern printing facilities, Bubar's "S.O.S. Foundation" is now one of the fastest-growing semi-religious organizations in the South.

"After only three and a half years as a professional psychic," Bubar said when discussing this phenomenal growth, "I now spend about three and a half hours per week on radio and an average of about one and a half hours per week on television. Add to this forty-two personal counseling sessions, answering between three to four hundred personal letters, meeting roughly three hundred visitors; declining one thousand casual counseling requests and fulfilling an average of three speaking engagements, *all in one week,* and you can see that the life of a professional psychic is not an easy one.

"Lately two new developments have added to my workload, but in a very meaningful way. This past summer we conducted the first of what will be a series of yearly psychic seminars—training sessions where psychic enthusiasts can become acquainted with the latest developments in the psychic realm. The second is the publication of a new tabloid entitled *Psychic Adventurer,* a monthly newspaper that will eventually go to the eighty thousand who are on our mailing list.

"Busy? Yes, but in a meaningful way, and that makes it all worthwhile."

Since our first meeting, demands on David Bubar's time have increased even more. Flashing his disarming smile, he readily admits that he may not as yet have uncovered the ultimate or total answer to many questions fired at him by those who stubbornly persist in trying to see "beyond," but he is equally certain that the answers given in this book present the best explanation, the most plausible theory and the most effective training method yet.

And there is no doubt; his personal approach brings results far greater than might be expected, for it helps create a deeper understanding of the unseen world of which many know so little and can see nothing at all.

The eyes of Bubar see "beyond" the boundaries of physical reality. How *far* and how *deep* are questions only *you* can answer.

Fairfax, Virginia   Rene Noorbergen
October 1970

CHAPTER ONE

With a sigh of exhaustion I put down the pen, leaned back and relaxed. Before me on the table lay the final presentation, the outline of the subject I would be discussing with the Spiritual Development Group in exactly forty-five minutes. Within my room all was quiet and serene, but one glance through the open window forced me to admit the presence of life's meaningless cadence. Worried faces and hurried footsteps passed by my window in an endless stream. The people were on their way home; they were aiming themselves in the direction of their overnight shelters. The results of their battles for survival could be felt in my room as their vibrations touched mine. The day was almost ready to join the yesterdays of the past and their haggard faces showed it.

I closed my eyes, and slowly, ever so slowly, allowed myself to drift inward—inward to the sanctity of the inner soul. Tranquillity closed in on me and with it came a sound, familiar, yet alien to the serenity of my mind. Louder and louder it sounded until it tore away the lacy curtain of Godly peace. Taking a deep breath, I swiveled in my chair, opened my eyes and reached for the ringing phone.

"This is David Bubar. May I help you?"

A worried voice broke in before I had finished.

"Yes, Mr. Bubar. This is Tommy Hutchinson in Munford, Tennessee. I heard you speak once in Huntsville, Alabama, and now I am really desperate. I need you. Will you help me?"

"I can't, Tommy, but God power can—"

Stunned silence encompassed the phone on the other end of the line. Then Tommy came back.

"God power? But I thought that—"

"Don't worry, Tom," I interrupted softly. "It is the power that directs everything in creation. You can't go any higher. It's the power I work with. Now what is your problem?"

"Well, it's like this. My sister, her husband and two children left last Wednesday for a vacation in Colorado Springs. Two days after they left, on Friday night to be exact, our brother dropped dead of a heart attack, and we can't locate them to tell her to hurry back. . . ." He groped for words, then blurted out, "Can you help us locate them?"

"God power can, Tommy. Let's work on it right now. First, please form a mental picture of your sister in your mind, inasmuch as she is closer to you than your brother-in-law. Have you got it? Can you see her? Now tell me her name, and pronounce it carefully and slowly."

"Yes, I have her in mind. Her name is Paula Jones."

"Please keep that mental picture right in focus. . . . Keep looking at it so I can probe the image. . . . Okay? Now tell me, is there anyone at their home at this moment?"

"Yes, their son is waiting by the phone just in case someone should call in."

"Have they been calling him every day since they've been gone?"

"No, not at all!"

"Would they be calling him for any reason?"

"Not that I can think of."

An idea suddenly crossed my mind. This would make an excellent project for the Spiritual Development Group that was to meet tonight. I didn't inform Tommy of my plan but urged him to cooperate in his own way.

"Tommy, Paula will call her home tonight between eight thirty and nine o'clock, but I need your assistance to make this possible. I want you to meet with someone else at that time, and I want the both of you to get a mental picture of her in mind. Then, I want you to think, not say but think, *'Paula, wherever you are, please call home at once. Call home at once. Go to the phone and call home at once.'* Do this over and over until your phone begins to ring. When you pick up the receiver, Paula will be on the other end.

"At that exact time, I will do the same thing here in Memphis. You can rest assured that she will call immediately."

When my Spiritual Development Group met twenty minutes later, I looked at them with tense anticipation. I knew that the power of sixty people requesting intervention by Divine Power would be almost unbeatable; however, I didn't tell them of the project until after the close of our study session.

"There is a man in trouble," I told them quietly. "And he has asked for our help.

"I have saved his need as a special project for our meeting tonight. Remember what I have said regarding the force of spiritual power? Well, tonight I am going to make you use it.

"Rest and meditate. I will give you the details when you are ready for them."

I sat down and waited.

Silence . . . complete unearthly silence drowned out every

word and whisper. I felt the power, the majesty of Super Guidance come over us.

I stood up and faced the group once again.

"Our problem tonight is to contact someone who is unaware that we are aiming our thoughts at her. Remember, your thoughts—your thought power—is like ammunition. You can direct your thoughts. Don't send them helter-skelter. Have a purpose, a direction for your thoughts.

"Aim them and intend to reach your goal!

"You are trying to reach Paula Jones. She is middle-aged and is at present with her husband in the vicinity of Colorado Springs. Her brother just died, and she must call home at once.

"Please think the name Paula Jones consciously and as powerfully as you can. Think the name and try to form a picture in your mind of a woman driving around Colorado Springs who goes by that name. Now, RELEASE your thoughts and imagine them traveling through the air in a straight line toward the Colorado Springs area. They will find her wherever she is.

"I want you to think with me: 'Paula Jones, wherever you are—please go to the phone and call home at once. Please, Paula, call home at once. It is urgent!'"

Anxious to test their newfound power and eager to help, the sixty people repeated the mental message over and over again, directing their thoughts to Colorado Springs and Paula Jones.

"If any of you feel that you have reached Paula, let me know."

For the group, it was a new experiment in mental communication, and I had decided to let them go it all alone with only the basic guidance necessary. I was certain that the results would encourage them to reach new heights in mental development.

Carol James was the first one to break the heavy silence.

"She has received me!" she exclaimed agitatedly, a blush of excitement rushing to her cheeks.

I nodded. Somehow I knew she would be the first one. Carol was a middle-aged woman who helped her mother in managing a florist's shop in Memphis, and even though she was a member of the Little Flower Catholic parish, she was also a regular member of these development sessions and had become quite sensitive to mental impressions.

A man cut in. "Yes," he said slowly, concentrating on what he was saying as though he were still following Paula's actions. "She has received the message and is picking up the phone right now."

I concluded the meeting. I knew the distance gap had been breached, and to allow the others to continue with their forced thought-beams would only lead to confusion.

"I am sure she has been reached, and I want to thank you for your participation. I will let you know the details of your contact as soon as I am informed."

A few moments later as the group was being dismissed for refreshments, the phone rang.

It was Tommy Hutchinson.

"She just called," he stammered, awestricken. "Paula just called. It happened just as you said it would. The whole family is so grateful for what you have done."

I then explained exactly what had happened and how his sister had reacted to the thought force of a group of sixty people. He remarked excitedly that Paula had phoned at the precise moment we had projected our request for her to call home.

The story, however, actually ended two days later when another member of the family called to express appreciation for the help.

"Paula and her husband were just checking into a motel

in Colorado Springs for the evening," she related, "when she felt a sudden urge to dash to a telephone and call home. And without even telling her husband, she slipped off to a phone booth while he was registering and called her son. He picked the phone up on the first ring, and when she heard the story of what had occurred, she and her husband hurriedly took the first flight out that night and reached Memphis in time for the funeral."

It was thought power, strengthened by God power, that had brought Paula home!

Most people express a polite and distant incredulity when confronted with proof of psychic power. More often, the psychic himself becomes the target of ridicule from those whose mental powers are still in the infant stage. The subject of parapsychology and related matters has never yet been fully investigated by scientists. Since no one has ever agreed to the establishment of a set of ground rules against which psychic phenomena can be judged or agreed to a basic vocabulary fitting these phenomena, the psychic often finds himself explaining not only his abilities and beliefs, but also the basic principles that are brought into play.

All this tends to create chaos in a world where misapprehension reigns supreme, and a psychic is more often than not confused with a carnival magician.

Man is inquisitive, and when answers are not readily available, new questions are inclined to pile on top of the old ones, creating a problem of ever-increasing dimensions. One question, however, that is invariably asked of every psychic—the answer to which is supposed to eradicate all doubt—is the most simple one of all. "How do you do it?" they ask. "How do you make your predictions? How do you explain your gift of ESP? How come you have it and I don't?"

The answer is the same for every individual. It is within reach of all.

Take ESP for example. To say that ESP, or as I prefer to call it "Energy Power," exists is like admitting that I have two hands, two feet and a head. I was born with them. They were not added on or optional. Neither, I believe, is perception, in any sense of the word. Humans, animals—yes, every living organism—have a degree of perception. It is just as much a part of us as is any physical part of our body. It is the extent to which it is consciously developed that can make it obvious.

The awareness or sensitiveness that many gifted people possess is natural to every living creature. However, and this tends to cause the prevailing confusion, some people are born with what appears to be an amazingly developed degree of psychic sensitivity, much like the baby who is born with thick long hair, while others don't seem to have any hair at all. Every human has the capability of knowing of things that have happened in the past or of feeling the vibrations of events still to take place.

Awareness and perception are inherent in every living being, but their scope and degree of sensitivity must be developed very much like the muscles of an athlete. Some of the world's leading vocalists were born with their beautiful voices; others worked long and hard to attain the same degree of perfection. Through diligent training, studying and perseverance they eventually became the equal of the ones born with it. In the field of psychic ability, things are very much the same.

I recall a friend who did not seem to have any musical ability whatsoever, yet he desperately wanted to become a concert pianist. He worked hard and studied deep into the night and ultimately won a Pepsi-Cola scholarship to one of our leading universities. Eventually he developed his inherent ability and could transform the pages of sheet music into heavenly melodies.

In the same way, you can develop your ability to feel. You can touch things—physical things—but feeling is a sense reserved for personal communication with emotions such as sorrow, love and the power of pure energy. Concentrate, and guided by the right principles, you can learn how to tune in to someone else's energy or can have your energy tune in or harmonize with someone else's. The mind is the physical component, the body, through which this energy operates. By beaming your energy outward and forcing it to probe energy projected by someone else, you can actually assume and feel the problems of that other energy's physical body.

Jim Alexander is a noted architect from Memphis, Tennessee. While studying at Memphis State University, he called me one day and shortly thereafter came to see me, for he had been told about my "unusual powers" (at least that is what someone called it). He was quite intrigued with these powers, and as I was walking him to the door at the close of our discussion, I asked him to stop for a moment.

I placed my hand on his lower abdomen.

"Have you ever had a hernia operation or an appendectomy?" I queried.

"No, in fact I've never had any symptoms that could be interpreted as such," he replied.

"You'd better see a doctor, Jim," I cautioned him, "for I feel both of them."

Early the next morning I left for Maine, the state where I spent my early years, to pass some time with my relatives. As I walked into my office upon my return three weeks later, a familiar sound greeted me. I reached for the ringing phone. It was Jim Alexander.

"I just got out of the hospital, David," he said, obviously still impressed by what I had previously told him. "Within two days after your warning, I had to go to the hospital for acute appendicitis, and while there, they also took care of a hernia I had developed.

"Dave, how did you feel what was going to happen?"

His question was the expected one under the circumstances, but his basic premise was wrong. I did not feel it. It was my outgoing energy that had touched his energy and found something amiss. I did not "feel" the operation with my own body, but my energy—much like radar—came back to me with the information that it was going to happen. Time is a difficult thing to judge in the sixth dimension where time and space do not exist, and when one works with the invisible, one works with this dimension. Yet, even though the operations were days away, the forefeeling of it was already present.

The forces projected from us can do more, much more. Often an inborn ability or gift needs only a catalyst to emerge into the open. The ableness to probe or search an individual's energy and have my vibrations return to me with the information was developed over a period of time, exploiting the ability that was already there.

This is the way I learned to play my first instrument. I can remember trying to play the old pump organ in my grandmother's home when I was only five years of age. My sister Rachel taught me to play "I love coffee, I love tea" as a reward for drying the supper dishes for her. The melody was simple, but it opened up unknown worlds to me. From the very first moment I touched the organ I began to "hear" music in my mind. Dreamy sultry melodies, floating through the air, filling every nerve of my body. Sheet music never meant anything to me. I either played a melody perfectly with all the fine touches normally reserved for the masters or just repeated the melodies I heard in my mind. At the age of thirteen I received a dollar a day for playing in church on Sunday. In later years I attended the University of Richmond and taught organ as a sideline, making more money teaching private organ lessons than the music professors at the university—yet I had never had a lesson. Still later while attending Louisiana State University and the New Orleans Seminary, I played entire organ concerts for capacity audiences. These performances were often based on the melodies that I heard in my mind, and my fingers would move gently over the keyboard in a familiar manner as though I had played that particular composition a hundred times before. More often than not, it was a new one every time.

It was in those years that I became more strongly aware of the power of radiated energy and the power of the energy of the mind. Many times while playing at a church service and becoming bored with the lengthy ecclesiastical prayers of the minister, I would direct thoughts to his mind, and soon he would be stumbling and stammering out the strange words that I was sending to him, often to his great embarrassment. On other occasions I would experiment and send him an "Amen," and invariably he would inject an abrupt "Amen" into his prayer and then feel too flustered to begin all over again. Other times my message would impress on him the thought to keep on praying without ceasing, and often the poor clergyman would pray incessantly until the pews would begin to creak and pop as restless parishioners shuffled painfully into new positions.

Having been brought up in a minister's home with four brothers who are now ministers, I found the church to be an ideal laboratory for psychic experiments and spiritual development. I can still recall a comical incident that occurred many years ago while I was a guest organist in a lovely dignified black church. At that time I was a student at Louisiana State University and was quite young and impetuous, possessing a mischievous sense of humor. Looking back now, however, I know that it was not the right place to conduct these particular tests, but in those days I looked at things differently. Having invited an old friend to come along and observe me at work in my "laboratory," we agreed that my signal for the start of the experiment would be a deliberate yet almost undetectable nod.

When the time came for the closing hymn, the minister walked toward the front of the pulpit and invited the congregation to come forth and dedicate themselves to the Lord. I began to play the hymn of invitation, "Pass Me Not O Gentle Savior," and gave my friend John the expected nod. Within seconds things began to happen. Suddenly the minister stretched forth his arms as if to fly away from his lofty perch. John sat in his pew frozen with disbelief. I continued my playing and kept the congregation going while Ole Rev tried to fly. Higher and higher stretched his arms, and with beads of perspiration racing down his weathered cheeks, he gently began to sway with the music. Proud of such a fantastic accomplishment I became careless, and with a wide smile on my face I turned toward my friend, who still sat nailed to his pew, and winked. At that moment a vigilant deacon caught sight of my smirk, leaped to his feet, rushed to the organ and grabbed hold of my arms.

"Stop that right now, you hear?" he whispered forcefully in my ear. "Stop it right now!"

Gently I shrugged off his arm and smiled innocently at the congregation as if I greatly appreciated what they thought was the deacon's compliment.

After the services concluded, the deacon, who also turned out to be a professor at Southern University came up to me, put his arm around my shoulder and smiled.

"I thought Ole Rev was going to drop from exhaustion before you were through with him," he grinned. "I don't know how you did it, son, but I know you did it."

Since that event, I have tried many times to explain to

various people what really happened that morning. I know he was not hypnotized, nor was he paralyzed and not in control of his body, yet a supernatural force had taken charge of him and made him react. It was my mind force that had taken over, and because it was consciously directed and stronger than that of the reverend's, it gained the upper hand.

From my earliest days of remembrance, I have been aware that within all living things there is something besides that which you can see with the physical eye.

I frequently recollect the registered sheep my grandmother raised on her farm. During the spring lambing season, I used to communicate quietly with the newborn lambs as though we were both speaking an audible language. A feeling of love grew between us that was inexplainable. I would pick up a little furry bundle of lamb and silently talk to it. No matter which lamb I held, it always seemed to know what I tried to do—it seemed to understand my inner feelings.

For many years now I have known that mind force, the waves of undetermined yet existing frequencies, can create a variety of reactions, depending upon the will and determination of the person who is directing the force. The greater the force or the ability of the person using the force, the greater is the ability to receive signals or vibrations emanating from other persons or beings. In many ways it can be compared to a well-tuned transmitter-receiving set. An expensive and well-adjusted unit can not only receive more stations, but can also reach further in its quest to broadcast its message to other receivers. This partly explains why psychics not only communicate easily with others, but also why telepathy and psychic messages are being received by them in a much greater quantity or frequency than by nonpsychics.

There have been sensitives throughout the ages of human history, yet this age seems especially ripe for the grand entrance of the psychics; for with the complexities of technology the problems of mankind have increased tremendously. Today people are searching for easy answers to their problems, and listening to a psychic or clairvoyant gives them that chance.

The psychic, however, can only relate what he feels or, if he is being a channel of communication, relay what he receives. I remember a short time ago, while flying on American Airlines from Memphis to Washington, my mind perfectly at rest, I became aware of soft music filtering into the plane. The higher we soared, the more majestic and regal the music resounded until, when we had reached our flying altitude, it suddenly burst into a grand crescendo of glorious voices and melodious harmony, creating music I never knew existed.

I stole a glance around me at the other passengers, but neither the gin rummy players in the corner nor the frightened couple in the seat next to mine seemed to realize what was happening. But the music kept on rolling in—wave after wave. Love, majesty, creation and sacrifice all became crystalline through the musical strains that took possession of me.

I quickly scrambled for my briefcase, fearful that I'd lose the music before I had an opportunity to record at least a portion of the score. Hurriedly I ripped open some old envelopes and drew staff lines on the back of the roughly torn pieces of paper. The music had become clearer now, possibly because our plane seemed to be climbing even higher. The orchestra had now completely blended and fused with the angelic choir. Pain and beauty, conflicting emotional reactions, embraced by music so tender yet so beautiful made my heart ache.

With tears glistening in my eyes, I grabbed for a pencil and began to write down the music as it came to me. Impressions of the Resurrection and eternal life were the overpowering themes that permeated the entire score. It was an Easter theme, and since it was but a month before Easter, I felt that this was only natural. I glanced at my seat partner. He quickly tried to conceal a pitying smile. He must have thought I was out of my mind. Here I was thousands of feet up in the air writing down music at a desperate pace.

Upon our arrival in Washington, D.C., the score was finished, and once back in Memphis, all that was necessary was to transfer it to better paper and give it to my church choir to sing for Easter Sunday.

The choir never received so many compliments as it did that day.

Going through this experience opened my eyes to something I should have been aware of before—that the human senses are much more inclined to receive outside impulses when far removed from the disturbing magnetic influences of the earth. Another example of this happened while I was flying aboard a plane from Little Rock, Arkansas, to Memphis, Tennessee. With the vivid memory of past psychic experiences while flying at high altitudes still in my mind, I somehow knew this flight too would probably affect me the same way.

We no sooner had reached our cruising altitude when my eyes were pulled to a lady sitting several seats ahead of me, on the opposite side of the aisle. All that was visible was the top of her head, yet the vibrations between us seemed to be so harmonious that I felt compelled to concentrate on her. Still staring at her, I pulled a few sheets of paper from the seat pocket in front of me and began to write, faltering at first, then flowingly and at a steady pace. I am not a writer; yet here I found myself composing children's poems; cute little rhymes, full of meaning and rhythm. I remembered thinking, "Is this what it is like to be a writer? Does it always come this easy?"

Disembarking from the plane in Memphis, I tried to find a

plausible excuse to approach the lady whose presence seemed to have inspired me to write the poems. As she passed me in the airport lobby, I approached her, smiling.

"Pardon me—please don't misunderstand me for speaking to you like this, however, I am curious about something. Are you a writer? I have the distinct impression that you have something to do with poetry!"

She nodded her head—holding her distance while at the same time indicating a willingness to talk.

"Yes, I write poetry." She didn't volunteer any more information.

"I am David Bubar. I live here in Memphis. What kind of poetry do you write?"

"Children's poems. Why? Are you a writer?"

"No, but I would like you to take a look at these poems and tell me whether they are any good." After saying this, I gingerly handed her my newly written poems.

"Where did you get these," she exclaimed angrily, scanning them with a furious intensity. "Who gave them to you?"

"Sit down. I'll tell you all about it. It was because of an inspiration that you may never have thought of . . ." and we sat down.

After giving her an account of my supersensitive experiences in high altitudes and telling her how I came to write these poems, she began to show a growing interest and finally opened up a large pad she had been carrying under her arm. She showed me the contents. *They were her own poems, but they were identical in every respect to the ones I had been writing on the plane.*

"I use these in my dance studio in Meridian, Mississippi," she explained. "It's part of a new program I am developing, teaching children to dance while using these verses."

How did I transcribe her verses so accurately? Did they come to me in symbols? Did I hear voices reciting them to me? These are but a few of the questions people have asked me as I retold this incident. The only way that I explained it was that I heard them; I saw the words form themselves in my mind. Some came on the wings of a melody, others just came into my mind in the exact way I wrote them down.

On numerous occasions I have sat beside people and told them things that shocked them beyond belief. One day as I was flying somewhere over Arkansas, I knew something was wrong the moment I glanced in the direction of the woman who was occupying the seat next to mine.

"You seem to be worried," I said, "but it's unfounded. Your brother isn't dead yet, and what's more, he won't die either."

"Do you know him?" she gasped.

"I do now," I remarked. "I feel that your brother had a heart attack, but it was a slight one. He has nothing to worry about. What's more, your mother is with him at the hospital."

Before leaving the plane, I gave her my address and told her to contact me if she ever felt the need. A week later I received a letter from her confirming what I had told her on the plane.

These experiences have convinced me that elevation can be important in sharpening the psychic awareness of a person. In order to capture my inspirations while flying about, I purchased a Norelco portable dictaphone and began carrying it with me in my briefcase. Often when people call me now to ask my advice concerning various problems, I urge them to wait a few days, knowing that I'll soon be flying again and that the answer will present itself more clearly at that time.

It has never failed yet.

This last experience taught me that psychic power, like God power, is wherever you *want* it. It is omnipresent. My early years, my "laboratory" experiments, my psychic development sessions—they were all essential consecutive phases in my steadily increasing supersensitivity. Whether there is a special relationship between God power and high places is a question that may never fully be answered. Yet there must be something about being at high altitudes that frees a person's mind from a veil of earthiness that shrouds him when he is earthbound. Heights, understanding on a "higher plane" and reaching new heights in spiritual perception undoubtedly go hand in hand, but the reason for this is still one of the unfathomable mysteries of the universe.

Someday I should like to probe deeper into the relationship between height and increased perceptiveness.

I feel it may open up entirely new areas of research.

CHAPTER TWO

On Monday, September 8, 1969, a shocked nation stared at the headlines in the morning papers with disbelief.

The dateline of the story was fresh and so was the tragedy.

Headlined "Dirksen Dead in Capital at 73," *The New York Times* became the spokesman for the nation when it broke the sad news to a stunned America.

"Everett McKinley Dirksen, the Republican leader of the Senate, died today at Walter Reed Army Hospital. He was 73 years old. A hospital spokesman said the Illinois senator died at 4:52 P.M., two hours after he sustained a sudden cardiac and respiratory arrest."

That evening in the privacy of my Memphis home, I heard the television newscaster solemnly announce the death of Everett Dirksen. Slowly I bowed my head. So it had finally come.

It all began on August 11, 1969, when I was a guest on WSM-TV's dynamic Judd Collins Show in Nashville. Judd, a real skeptic when it comes to dealing with psychics, didn't try to conceal his doubt from me or from his live audience, who fully expected him to tear me apart in the established Judd Collins fashion.

"Now, David, really," he started, jabbing at me with well-aimed sarcasm, "if there is *really* something to this psychic bit"—and with that he turned to face his ever-loyal fans, giving them his all-knowing, sarcastic, cynical smile, and turning back to me again continued—"then how about making a prediction for us right here on this show? Just *one* prediction in front of all of our viewers, so that we can all check on the possible outcome."

To me, there was no doubt now; Judd was convinced I was a fake and defied me to prove otherwise, feeling certain that either I would not dare or that my prediction would fall flat on its face. He had been dealing with a number of pseudo-clairvoyants on his show in the past, and his skepticism had won the upper hand.

"Well now, Judd," I said, "you know I'll be speaking at the Andrew Jackson Hotel tonight—why don't you curb your curiosity and wait until you can hear my predictions tonight?"

Judd cut me short. "But David, you claim to have the power to make predictions. *If you do*, then how about making just one on this show?"

Credibility gap? Intelligence gap? I had better perform, because he was out to draw blood.

Irritated by his dogged insistence, I raised my hand and shook my finger in his face.

"Judd Collins," I spoke pointedly, "if you want a prediction right now, then I will make you one," not having the slightest idea at the time of what I was going to say, "I will make you a prediction that you can check on. I'll make one so obvious and so easy to verify that when you see it come true in the newspaper headlines, you'll realize I knew what I was talking about."

"My prediction . . ." and suddenly it came, the words forcing themselves on Judd in rapid succession, "deals with a man in Washington. This man is *very close* to the President, but he *is not* the President. He is also very close to the Vice-President, yet it is not him either. The man I am speaking about is a very good man, a very humble man. He is what I would call a statesman rather than a politician. This man has a deep gravel-toned voice and an abundance of hair. He is extremely well known. This man will be dead within thirty days."

I stopped, for suddenly I realized that I had been describing Senator Everett Dirksen, the Republican leader of the Senate.

"Want to tell us who he is?" Judd probed still further.

"No Judd, I can't. I'd rather not, but I hasten to add that his death will be a violent one, almost as cruel as an assassination. It will be a very sad death, and you will all know about it."

Some time later in the refreshing air outside the studio building, the true impact of what I had just foretold hit me. I knew my prediction had nothing to do with the cause or the timing of the senator's death, yet I had given away sufficient clues to enable the curious to glue the pieces together and come up with the right name, and this I regretted. Psychic impressions that reach me are often so detailed that anyone grasping all the facts can readily arrive at the only correct conclusion or identification. I frequently suppress many of these facts when relating the psychic impression of a pending tragedy, because a large percentage of these are revelations of destiny; and a warning, however well intended would be of little use. To tell or not to tell is a decision that is mine alone, and it isn't always an easy one to make.

Contrary to the work of some other well-known psychics,

I do not study political trends and business reports to arrive at my predictions after careful scrutiny of blatantly obvious indications. Mine come spontaneously—as will be discussed in another chapter—however, when they emerge and demand attention, they deserve it.

As if my ominous forecast concerning Senator Dirksen wasn't sufficient for one day, my evening appearance at the Andrew Jackson Hotel produced others; one of which was as startling in its own way as the Dirksen prediction.

"The Russians will make alarming news in connection with their space program," I spoke out that night, "by putting three objects into space that will be new and completely different from anything else they have launched thus far. *I 'psych' the three objects fusing to become one giant spaceship.* It will be a first of its kind and even though many people in the United States will regard this as proof that we are lagging behind in the space race, this is not true. The Russian program has been established so as to arrive at the same ultimate goal only along a different approach.

"This Russian 'space first' will take place anywhere from around the middle of October until the first of November."

As it turned out, my prediction missed the Russian space-first by only a day and a half, for on October 13, (not 15 as I had predicted), Associated Press carried the following teletype newsflash:

"Soviets Expand Orbital Flights—Three Spaceships Now Carrying 7 Cosmonauts May Form Permanent Station.

"Moscow, October 13—(AP). *Seven Soviet cosmonauts— the biggest assembly of men in space at one time—hurtled around the Earth in three spacecrafts Monday, apparently getting ready to put together the first permanent orbiting space station.*

"Soyuz 8, piloted by two veteran spacemen, blasted off from the Baikonur cosmodrome in Soviet Central Asia earlier

in the day to join Soyuz 6 and Soyuz 7, sent aloft Saturday and Sunday.

"Official announcements were vague about the Soyuz trio's mission. But semiofficial sources said the spacecraft would link up after Soyuz 8 had been checked out by its crew."

Even though the printed record of my space forecast may have gotten lost among the millions of news items that unceasingly bombard the American public every day, there is a definite indication that it was cut out and carefully stored by researchers working with ESP in Eastern Europe and Russia. For at the time of this writing, fourteen government-sponsored and directed ESP Research Centers are in operation throughout Eastern Europe and the USSR. Their reports of psychic phenomena and happenings taking place the world over are collected and evaluated, because the Russians are considering the use of ESP as a military weapon and as a sophisticated means of communication with intelligent beings that possibly exist in other solar systems. Their reaction to our unofficial experiments in America and to published occurrences is not known; however, the advance knowledge of their space exploits to a number of American sensitives must be gratifying to them, for they are extremely interested in long-distance telepathic communication. My receiving their country's planned space experiments somehow proves at least the existence of extrasensory communication.

Although not every psychic impression I receive is noteworthy, some capture the headlines because their fulfillment is too precise to be ignored.

One of these, undoubtedly, was the water landing of a Japanese airliner in San Francisco.

The date was November 21, 1968, and I had just concluded the more formal portion of my speech to a group at the Holiday Inn in Memphis, Tennessee. While answering a question from one of the women in the audience, I was suddenly struck by an impression of airplanes. They surrounded her in such organized profusion that there seemed to be a system, a method to it.

When I confronted her with this, she smiled.

"I work at an airport, Mr. Bubar," she replied. "In fact, I work in the control tower."

"Hold on," I interrupted her. "There's something wrong here. I see an airplane that's out of place. It upsets the entire balance. It is a large one, and I know it should be on the runway, but it is not. It appears to be resting on a big patch of grass all around the plane. Yes . . . it is getting clearer now. This plane does not belong to our country and has unusual markings on it and strange numbers and designs. I see the significance of this plane all around you. Here, let me read the numbers to you—" and I proceeded to read her the plane's identification numbers. "Watch out for this. You will soon know about it in more detail, very soon!"

The outcome hurriedly caught up with the prediction, for the following day, Wallace Turner, special correspondent of *The New York Times,* filed this story:

"SAN FRANCISCO, November 22—107 Safe as Jet Hits Bay in West. *A Japan Air Lines DC-8 jet came down in San Francisco this morning about three miles short of the runway at International Airport.*

"*The craft, its wheels down, settled on a mud bank. The 96 passengers and 11 crewmen aboard climbed into rubber rafts and were towed to a yacht basin dock about 700 yards away. No injuries were reported.*

"*'We made a perfect water landing,' said Dudley Scholte of Bronxville, N.Y. 'If you want a water landing, we made a perfect one.'*"

I checked into the crash after the prediction became a reality and was told that by looking down from the tower onto the shallow waters of the bay, the water actually appears to be green, and the plane laying on the sand bank seemed to be resting on a soft coat of grass.

And then there was Ike Miller . . .

My relationship with Ike began in the year 1964, when I visited an acquaintance, Dave Early, in Eureka, California. His brother-in-law Joe Jessel was reputed to be a faith healer, and desperate people from both the United States and Canada continuously sought his help. One such man, who was searching for a cure for his arthritis, was Ike Miller.

I fail to recall why Ike happened to be at the Earlys that day, but I was with him only a few moments when I noticed silver all around him.

I told him. He grinned widely, tobacco juice dripping down the corners of his mouth.

"I've been a prospector and a jack-of-all-trades most of my life," he confessed proudly. "I'll be eighty-three on January 24; and you name it, and I've been there and done it!"

I sat down beside the old miner and concentrated on him.

"I notice several pieces of property in connection with you," I told him, and went on to describe each one of them to the minutest detail. "Two of these lots are in a mountainous region, and I see a heavy silver vein running up through the mountain." We talked some more about prospecting in general, and when we parted company late that evening, I thought our discussion was finished; that is, until he called me a few months later from somewhere in British Columbia.

"I got me some old maps of this mountain terrain up here," he shouted excitedly over the phone, "and want to mail them to you. I have a feeling there's a lot of silver up here. Can you take a look at the maps and mark the spots for me?"

Not long after our conversation I received the maps. Silver veins ran in all directions. With a thick crayon, I carefully marked several x's on the maps and mailed them back to Ike.

Shortly thereafter I received another phone call from Ike.

"Got the maps, David." He could be heard chuckling. "You must be quite something. Your x's are just about where I'd figured the silver must be. What now?"

"Jump, Ike, jump on it!" I said as forcefully as I could. "There *is* a lot of silver up there, but you'll be too late if you don't charter a helicopter today—right now—and go to stake your claim. Tomorrow will be your last chance. Saturday will be too late. File those claims tomorrow or forget it!"

Without a moment's delay, Ike chartered his helicopter, staked his claims and filed them the very next day. How fortunate that he did, too, for the following day headlines screamed about one of the largest silver strikes in British Columbia's history and in precisely the same area. Within hours, eager prospectors were crawling all over the mountains with their picks and shovels at the ready, staking claims left and right and swearing their dearest oaths when stopped by Ike Miller's claims.

But that was not all. In the evening a short few weeks later as I was having a sandwich and orange juice with Charles Goodman, a local journalist friend, and Dr. Harvey Reese, a psychiatrist, the phone rang. Ike was on the other end of the line.

"I'm rich, David!" he hollered enthusiastically into the phone. "I've struck it rich. Remember the mountain you said was on one of the claims? Well, it's an artificial mountain. It is a huge pile of silver ore! This pile was formed when overhead lines of buckets from another mining operation passed above this piece of land years ago sloshing some of the ore from the buckets as they made a sharp turn. In time a huge pile of ore has built up, and now it's mine!"

"How high is the pile of ore?" I asked.

"About seventy-five thousand tons of it," Miller replied.

"How much do you think it's worth?"

His reply was filled with worry-free excitement.

"I had several assays made of it," said Miller. "One assayed at $20.41 a ton, another at $16.93 a ton, still another at $29.60 a ton, but the last one beat them all with an appraisal of $42.39 a ton."

"How much will this add up to?"

Miller replied in a hushed tone, "There's over one million dollars' worth of ore lying there, David," and with a voice choked with emotion he added, "I am rich, David. I'm rich! It's finally happened!"

Several years ago, on November 9, 1967, as reported in the Delta *Democrat Times*, I voiced for the first time a strong psychic impression which focused on the future of American church life.

"The Christian Church as you know it today will cease to exist," I predicted with a sad note of regret. "It is crumbling and disintegrating. Within three to five years the established Church will have disappeared. Christ, however, will never disappear, nor the Christians, but we have made the tragic mistake in attempting to make God in our image.

"Don't blame your ministers; the things they would like to do but cannot are caused by your own inability and ignorance.

"Within the next five years you will witness the greatest revolution in religion, making social revolutions seem like nothing at all. Many of our church buildings will become monuments and museums as they are in Russia today.

"The Catholic Church will undergo a drastic overhaul and will take on an entirely different face. Protestantism and Catholicism will once again merge. I foresee the day when there will be only one centrally organized church which will become the mother church. . . . It will be surrounded by a small number of determined separatists and fundamentalists.

"Religion will adopt a new image and will become a way of life!"

When I first predicted this transformation in our religious life, it was greeted with hilarious laughter. The pipe dream of ecumenical unity was going to be the salvation of the Church, or so everyone thought; but now, a mere three years later, the laughter has died down, and justly so.

In a feature article of the March 23, 1970 issue of *U.S. News & World Report* appeared the following statements, pointing toward a rapid and almost literal fulfillment of my three-year-old forecast.

Headlined "Why Churches Are Worried," the magazine story lists among others the following facts: Talking about the developing crisis in the Church, it says, "One estimate circulated rather widely is that at least 3,000 Protestant ministers, or 1 per cent of the total, are leaving the vocation each year, and perhaps 2,500 Roman Catholic clergymen, or 4 per cent of all priests in the U.S. are dropping out annually. Thousands of nuns also are leaving religious life."

The Yearbook of American Churches, published by the National Council of Churches, shows that the total number of clergy in all denominations declined from 402,000 in 1967 to 360,000 in 1969. During that time the number of clergymen holding down pulpits declined even more, from 263,000 to 198,000.

Any more laughter? Perhaps, but surely not from my

critics, who called my 1967 prediction the most ridiculous thing they'd ever heard!

Throughout my life, predictions have come to me without previous warning, but not everyone reacts in a friendly way when confronted with them.

Years ago while attending school in Richmond, Virginia, I spent an evening at the home of Reverend and Mrs. Leland (Manny) H. Waters. In those days, he was the executive secretary of the Baptist Council of Richmond, and as such, was highly respected. Psychic phenomena became the subject of our evening's discussion, and during the course of the conversation, Mrs. Waters and a woman whose husband owned the Virginia Tour Bus Lines pressed me for psychic impressions concerning them and persons close to them.

I closed my eyes tightly, concentrated and began to "psych" a rose, a beautiful red rose, and with it one lonely, dirty shoe.

Laughter greeted my ears when I told them about it. "I'm frankly puzzled about this combination," I remarked. "The rose means love; it pertains to someone who is close to one of us here, but the shoe . . ." I shrugged my shoulders in a gesture of defeat, "I don't know what to tell you, but if this helps at all, I also see an airplane, but the connection is still not clear."

Four days later, the woman's son was killed in an Air National Guard plane crash. His remains were never found. The only identifiable object left of him after the crash was a solitary dirty shoe, and it was this shoe that was buried with full military honors.

On the coffin lay a bouquet of long-stemmed red roses —a token of his mother's love.

A few nights after this tragic mishap, I found myself again

sitting around the table at the Waters home, when suddenly I began to smell smoke.

I grabbed for a napkin and simultaneously yanked a pen from my coat pocket.

"I smell smoke, Manny," I hurriedly interrupted his conversation. "Here, let me draw it for you and show you where the fire is."

Unfolding the napkin to its fullest, I quickly began to sketch a building and positioned the windows where I sensed them to be.

"This is it! This is the building, and it's on fire. It's completely engulfed in flames. I can see sparks. I hear the dry crackling sound of burning wood. I smell burning paint and gasoline. Hold it, I see airplanes. Three airplanes are parked in this building, and they're burning up—they're on fire!" I shouted.

All conversation ceased, and the room became deathly still. Everyone stared fixedly at my face, particularly one Major Leland Waters, son of Reverend Waters, who was an officer in the Virginia Air National Guard and private pilot of the then governor of Virginia, Governor Tuck Cox.

He laughed loudly and conspicuously and was just ready to make a snide remark when the phone rang.

Reverend Waters answered it and called to his son.

The expression on Major Waters's face underwent a change from disgust over my "performance" to pure astonishment and fright as he listened intently to the voice on the other end of the line. White and shaken, he slammed down the receiver and slowly but deliberately walked up to me.

He flung out his hand and shook an angry finger in my face.

With eyes blazing, he shouted at his father, "Get that 'thing' out of here. Get him out of here. How can he know what's happening? This call was from Byrd Field. One of our hangars is on fire, and three planes have already been burned. Get that thing out of here!"

Needless to say I went—and fast!

Being a close witness to human tragedy involving friends or relatives of friends, as I was with Major Waters, isn't the most effective way to win a popularity contest. Sometimes this feeling of precognition can hurt in a real physical way, especially when it forecasts the death of a dear, dear friend.

On a Monday evening not so long ago, Martha Kosanke, author of *Light of Truth,* was in Greenville, Mississippi, to speak to a group at the home of Rusty Frayser, a veteran in the book business whose wife was on the staff of one of the local newspapers.

At a reception staged afterward, I noticed among the guests my old friend Dr. C. P. Parker. During the course of the evening, I felt an urgent need to walk over and talk earnestly and at length with him, yet the reason for this was unknown to me. I just felt we had to have a man-to-man talk, but nothing came of it.

The reception was a long, dragged-out affair, and when it was over I hurriedly gathered my things together in order to rush that night to Jackson to attend a retreat starting the next day.

While I was leaving the house, Dr. Parker forced his way through the guests milling near the doorway and touched me on the arm.

"David, I have to see you. I must . . . There are some things you and I have to talk about."

Parker was getting older. Wearing black horn-rimmed glasses and partially bald, he was tall in stature, strong and sturdy, yet he had aged considerably, and that night he showed every one of his days.

I hadn't seen him for quite some time, but when he approached me outside the house, he was not the same Dr. Parker I had seen inside. This one was dead—all I could see around him was death—a pale green death. I felt like crying.

Frightened by what I saw, I stretched out my arm wanting to keep him at a distance.

"I've got to run now, Dr. Parker," I managed to stammer, "but when I return I will call you and we'll have that long talk."

The shimmering green color surrounding him began to fade. I turned and carefully inched closer to Dr. John Sutphin, Chairman of the Department of Philosophy and Religion at the University of Mississippi in Starkville.

"It's time to go now, Doctor," I said hastily and hurried along the walkway.

I felt weakened and drained, but the memory of that color stayed with me all the way to Jackson.

That night climaxed my premonition concerning the death of Dr. Parker, confirming my earlier suspicions about his approaching death. Several times I jumped out of bed, uneasy and perspiring, and paced the floor with tenseness, feeling that something was about to happen that I should be aware of, yet wasn't. Finally after many restless hours, I lapsed into my subconscious being and became a participant in the dream that had been awaiting me for all those countless minutes.

It seemed as though I were looking down on myself. I first noticed a saddened group of people entering a church, and I could pick myself out with unerring accuracy. There was someone with me. I tried to see his face, but it was obscured from my vision. Then I saw what I was doing. I was sitting on a bicycle, grasping a large bouquet of roses in my arm. Then I observed myself proceeding into the church and returning empty-handed. It became apparent that I must have left the roses inside, because the crowd that trailed behind me had come with nothing, yet now they were all leaving too, each one of them holding a single rose, smiling at it tenderly while cupping it gently in his hands.

My eyes were wet when I awoke, and a deep unfathomable grief possessed me as I walked down to the breakfast table.

"What's wrong, David?" my host queried when he detected my uneasiness.

"Someone very near to me is about to die," I answered, sad and distressed. "It has to be someone close, very close to me, otherwise it would not affect me this way." Deep inside I didn't want to believe that it would be Dr. Parker, for he was the one I had selected to work with me as an associate in the psychic-research project I had been planning. It just couldn't be *him*.

Suddenly and without warning as I was preparing to leave the table, the full impact of my premonition hit me. "The man who will die within the next fifteen or twenty minutes—" I cried out. "It's Dr. Parker—he will die— Oh no!" In an instant, it all became crystal clear; the grim reality of my dream now penetrated. The church I had seen was that of Dr. Parker, with its unmistakable tall pillars in front and the side entrance you must pass through when entering the church. In my dream I had carried the roses into the church through a side door.

With a heavy heart, I boarded a plane to fly back to Memphis via Greenville, Mississippi, where the flight was scheduled for a short stopover. We had scarcely taxied up to the terminal building when an airline official boarded the plane.

"I have a message for Reverend Bubar. There is an urgent telephone call for Reverend Bubar."

I hurried inside and grabbed the phone from the ticket

agent's hand. My host of the night before could be heard on the other end of the line.

"It was as you expected, David," he began breathlessly, breaking the news as softly as he could. "Dr. Parker died this morning as he started to get out of bed. He complained of a sudden pain and fell back on his bed. He died in his wife's arms. We just received the news from his home in Shaw, Mississippi."

Can anyone still presume that the life of a psychic is an easy one?

As a sensitive, one is apt to get involved with a variety of events and worthy causes, ranging from helping to raise money for an orphanage to assisting in the discovery of a solution for hitherto unsolved crimes. The crime angle entered my life while I was attending the funeral of my father in Waterville, Maine, in July, 1967.

The little metropolis of Old Towne had two recent unsolved murders on its hands, and Labrie Otis, Old Towne's chief of police, had clearly reached the limit of his ability in handling the current situation. I had been out of touch with local affairs in Maine for a number of years, but the fear and anxiety that had Old Towne in its grip was perceptible —the town's tranquillity had been disturbed. After the funeral, when I had a chance to meet with District Attorney Bernard Cratty and heard about the murders, I immediately offered my help.

"Just get a pad of paper," I suggested to him as we sat in his office that evening, "and I will try to describe some events surrounding the crimes." Concentrating deeply on the fear-ridden atmosphere that hung over the town, impressions began to form, and I was able to describe the manner in which the body of Cyrus Everett and later that of Donna Mauck had been found. I also disclosed details of their last hours with such precision and accuracy that

Bernard Cratty headed straight for Chief Otis's office and confronted him with my psychically gained information. "Where in hell did you get your information from?" a distraught chief of police muttered from under a suspicious stare. "Who has been reading my files? You've got facts there that I haven't told anyone about."

All possible angles of the cases were discussed, but no conclusions or decisions were reached at that time. My information was of scarcely any help to them, perhaps because they had so little faith in the word of a psychic. That winter, however, brought me back to Maine again, accompanied this time by my brother Benjamin, who incidentally is the executive secretary of the Christian Civic League in Maine.

We paid Labrie Otis another visit.

"I have come to help you shed some new light and discover some new clues to the murders of Cyrus Everett and Donna Mauck," I said, and added vehemently, "but I need your help, too!"

Labrie jumped up, a smile of relief spreading quickly over his otherwise unyielding countenance.

"The case was dropped a while back for lack of result, but I'll cooperate." And so we started.

It was noon on an overcast, blustery day when I tramped through the freshly fallen snow into a deserted swamp area on the border of Fort Fairfield, the small Maine town where the body of Cyrus Everett had been found. I had driven up to the marshland together with my brother Ben, who by this time was feeling quite ill at ease. Even though it was high noon, he felt nervous and jittery about visiting the site of a recent murder, especially since the local townspeople had no idea as to the reason for our activities and might attempt to detain us from searching for clues, thinking perhaps we were curiosity seekers.

Ben remained with the car while I walked what seemed

to be the equivalent of two or three city blocks penetrating far into the depths of the murky swamp. Darkness closed in on me, and I suddenly realized that I had reached the spot where Cyrus Everett had died. I stopped.

Briskly rubbing my shivering face with gloved hands, I tried to bring some heat to my numbed body, and gazing over that desolate swamp my thoughts were of Cyrus.

I closed my eyes and prayed.

"Father," I prayed, "here on this tragic spot, please pull back the curtains of my mind. Reveal to me what I have come here to know. Grant me insight and knowledge to know who committed this gruesome crime so that he can be brought to justice."

Within an instant, I was cognizant of all the facts. It seemed as though I could hear Cyrus describing the events leading up to the killing, the agony of his last moments on earth. I felt as though I were an integral part of all the circumstances that climaxed the final death scene in the swamp, and gasping for breath, I stumbled from that spot stricken by so much senseless violence.

Dazed, I staggered back through the snowy wilderness, crossed the field and climbed into the front seat of my brother's car, which he had kept running for warmth. Ben stared at me without saying a word. With numb fingers, I flipped the snow out of the cuffs of my pants, took off my shoes and socks and held my feet underneath the heater.

"Don't utter a sound, Ben," I pleaded softly. "Let me concentrate. I've got to figure this thing out."

I continued to think of Cyrus and of the house in which his murder and that of Donna Mauck were assumed to have been committed. We drove past the house that morning following an interview with Cyrus's mother, and it seemed incredible that two ghastly murders had possibly been committed behind the friendly facade of that two-story white frame house. But I now realized that my first conclusions had been correct. Both murders had *not* been committed there, for Cyrus had still been alive when moved from the house and dumped in the swamp.

Now the facts became clear to me. I could see how it all happened. The tragic series of events was touched off when Cyrus, on his paper route, had stopped by the white frame house to collect his paper money. With a gruff voice, the man had invited the boy inside the house, whereupon he had suddenly molested him—going completely beserk—and had ended up by grabbing a heavy object and striking the semiconscious boy on the back of the head.

It was dusk, and under cover of the fading sun, he had dragged the dying boy to a barn located about twenty feet from the house and left him there until the darkness of night closed in, concealing his suspicious movements from the preying eyes of the outside world. He then moved the boy again to a deserted swamp area, where he hid him under a log. There Cyrus, with a serious brain concussion, was left to die, but not before his money pouch, a pair of mittens and some Christmas cards had been removed from his body by the deranged killer.

For a short period of time, the murderer was committed to a mental hospital for treatment, and it was during this period that Donna Mauck picked up the thread that led to her death. Not wanting to lose revenue, the owners of the vacant house rented it to Donna Mauck for the duration of the former occupant's illness. After moving into the house, Donna must have discovered incriminating evidence such as the missing Christmas cards, the money pouch or the mittens, indicating that indeed the boy had been there. It was apparent that she realized she had stumbled on something, for she confided to her mother on the day prior to her death that she felt her life was in danger. I sense that it was the murderer who phoned the restaurant where Donna was on the evening of her death and left word to have her go home at once. "It is urgent!" the caller had said. "Please have her rush home."

Again my psychic impressions have given me the conclusion to this story. I feel that after completing the call, the murderer hid himself in the house, certain that Donna had found evidence linking him to the slaying of Cyrus Everett. After she opened the door, Donna Mauck never knew what happened. Police reports indicate that she, too, was struck with a blunt instrument and then dumped behind the sofa.

Where is the murderer now?

I have turned my impressions over to the proper authorities, together with the name of the killer. A full-scale investigation into the activities of that man on the days of the two murders will give the police sufficient facts for a conviction.

Often, while counseling, guiding or working with people to help solve their problems or even in relaying my psychic impressions to them, I wonder how they really look at me. "What would I think if I could look at David Bubar through their eyes?" I have repeatedly asked myself, and the answer does not easily present itself. Many psychics have gained their reputations by forecasting startling and tragic international occurrences. I prefer to keep mine in the realm of the personal and out of the sphere of political happenings.

How does a psychic feel? How do I feel? The answer is as difficult to explain as it would be to reveal the feeling of an inner emotional experience. It is impossible to reduce a psychic or the ability of a psychic to a workable formula in the same manner as you would reduce a mathematical problem to a typewriter equation. Undoubtedly the reason for this is that we are talking about something that is still regarded as weird and unknown by many researchers. To admit to the existence of psychic forces that are unexplainable, to agree to work with something that cannot be seen, heard or felt but only experienced, goes beyond the accepted norms of human behavior and understanding.

When I think of psychic forces, I think of energies. I am firmly convinced that all psychic phenomena, supernatural happenings and otherwise unexplained manifestations are the result of the working of thus far unmeasured electronic energy forces. These forces operate on frequencies never yet seen, never yet measured.

Their place of origin is a realm far beyond man's imagination, but their effectiveness is real beyond a doubt.

No scientist will deny the fact that man, being composed of atoms, has within him a tremendous source of energy. It is not, however, the human atom that fascinates me personally, but the proton, that particle which is the nucleus of the hydrogen atom and a constituent of the nuclei of other atoms. It is known to carry with it a positive charge. Conservative estimates place the electric potential of a single proton at 50,000 volts. *Can you imagine the tremendous electric potential we all carry with us, considering that a moderate calculation puts the number of protons in the human body at 50,000,000,000,000,000,000?* It is a frightening potential, for theoretically it would mean that every human individual is an electric powerhouse, harboring at least 2,500,000,000,000,000,000,000,000 volts of electric power. True, we are not as yet at liberty to release even a small portion of this potential at will, but One Who is greater than all of us once said that if we only had the faith of a mustard seed, we would be able to move mountains—and it is faith and ability that will eventually teach us how to release the harnessed energy sources within us.

Can you imagine what we might be able to do if we could learn how to release the power of only ONE proton? Let's take a finger, for example. The number of energy-packed protons in ONE finger runs into the billions, but we use not one of them in our eternal quest for power and understanding—yet it's there, waiting for us to release it!

Recent discoveries of the Backster Research Foundation in New York prove without the shadow of a doubt that even the most minute living cell emits intelligent signals. Emotional reactions of animal and plant cells can now be measured, traced and identified, and every one of these signals responds to external stimuli in such ways that we know now that intelligent life within those cells controls these signals. Now let the skeptics have their day and claim that only we humans have intelligence. Backster's records prove otherwise. To me, this discovery establishes the fact that all energy is closely connected to or is identical with intelligence. Energy is what keeps us together, and all our cells, atoms and protons scream for understanding. They plead to be heard—to be *used!* The human mind has the ability not only to release some of the locked-up power of these cells, but also to act as the only transmitter in establishing intelligent communication between various forms of God's creation. It is up to us to switch it on.

Let's get down to practical examples.

Can man ever learn how to control the basic elements of life? According to the Bible, the possibility exists. Jesus walked on the water (Matthew 14:25), completely mastering the atoms; He fed the multitudes when there was hardly food available (Matthew 16:9,10) increasing cells at a staggering rate of speed. He knew the innermost secrets of the woman He met at the well (John 4:18) and thereby demonstrated His command over the boundaries of the mind. He increased the wine needed for a wedding feast at Cana (John 2:7-11).

The Old Testament, too, is filled with examples of divine

intervention in the affairs of men, relating to the power God allowed men to possess in dealing with matters of state and of the people.

And gloriously tying this all together is a statement in the New Testament where Jesus says that "He that bequeath on me the works that I shall do, he shall do also; and greater works than these shall he do" (John 14:12), admitting to the ability of us all to perform "wonders" if our hearts and minds are tuned in to the God power of the universe.

Since the beginning of time, our knowledge has undergone a continuous process of expansion, culminating in modern-day technological society, owing to the fact that we have gained knowledge as to the utilization of some of the powers of the mind in uncovering hitherto undisclosed information that has been stored for us in the computer banks of eternity. The technological age is well underway, but once again humanity stands on the threshold of new discoveries; this time concerning the power of the mind, not merely the imagination of man. I firmly believe that the day will come when everyone will know exactly how to use these subconscious energies and not just talk about them. The turning point is now. Mind energy and God-given power (God power) is yours for the asking, but what will you do with it once you have captured the technique and have acquired a faith strong enough to know that God will entrust you with His Power when needed?

There are certain fundamentals that should be carefully considered before anyone decides to take the giant step leading to the development of one's psychic powers, for the accompanying responsibilities are great. Before you even start, you must determine whether you are fully prepared to face the difficulties you will encounter along the way and whether you are really willing to work and wait and persevere in your newfound quest for the maturation of your innermost power in spite of the adversities that will seek you out. Are you willing to sacrifice yourself for the sake of mental progress? It is a question that no one can answer but you—but the moment you have given yourself a satisfactory answer, pile another question on top of the first one: "Am I doing it to increase my own knowledge so that I can help others, or is it just curiosity that drives me to pursue it?" The answer could make the difference between success and failure.

Let us assume that you do have the right motivation to unharness the God-given energies within you, but that the knowledge and ability is the one thing that keeps you from exploiting these forces. There remains then one all-important question, "How do I unlock these powers of the mind?" It is here that God power enters into your life.

Realizing that all life has energy within it and that energy is a form of intelligence, we have to establish the right method of communication with our inner power, sparked by the right motivation. When Christ commanded the storm to cease (Mark 4:39), the winds obeyed His voice, because He was master over all. He knew how to communicate with energy, for God is Love, and Love is the strongest energy force known to man. Love is more than just a kissing game; you can't see it, yet you can feel it. Its frequency spans oceans; it is like a radiant but invisible beam of electromagnetic energy connecting one person to another.

Our inability to see electromagnetic frequencies is compensated for by our ability to recognize their effect. For example, take the frequency of light. With a speed of 186,-000 miles per second it penetrates windows, but because of its tremendous velocity, it passes through without shattering the glass. Now take the same beam, concentrate it by forcing it through a ruby, and you will have at your disposal a highly dangerous weapon known as the laser beam. Take *this* beam, aim it at an object of lower vibrations (a solid object), and it will disintegrate it. The higher vibrations have the ability to penetrate lower vibrations and accomplish that for which they were created.

Now human beings will learn how to use this energy force within themselves as they learn how to love. Vibrations play a much more important role in our society than we often realize. Discord and love are not just two words with opposite meanings. Discord has the effect of lowering the vibrations that abound when people are gathered together, creating a feeling of uneasiness, distrust and often outright hostility, but love has the quality of increasing the existing frequency, creating just the opposite effect. It is the absence of love that creates most of the world's problems. Love is the only key that can unlock our inner power and free us from the discords that have held us captive for so long.

If God is a perfect God—and we do believe that He is—and He has made man in His image and has empowered this creation with a free will, then why should we accept anything short of perfection? Why not use these energy forces if they can help us attain that which has been made almost unreachable by "worldly" vibrations? We should be busying ourselves to reach a state of perfection so that matter (that's us) can send forth the radiant energy of love to conquer the vibrations of pain and suffering. Christ demonstrated that He did not only resist disease, but that He could heal every type of disease including those that resulted from possession by evil spirits.

He knew how to control and utilize the forces of Good.

Today, man again is rediscovering the principles of energy. Not only are microwave ovens replacing the familiar gas or electric stoves, but compare the advantages of jet travel with those of the horse and buggy and it becomes obvious that something has changed drastically. Atomic power is more and more supplanting the hydroelectric and coal-burning power plants. One discovery leads to another, yet man has not as yet *touched* the rim of God's knowledge. In the future, many of the present-day medical techniques will no doubt become obsolete, because man will learn to use the energies within himself. Then, when a doctor has to treat a broken wrist, all he may have to do is place his own hand over the broken limb and through willpower divert some of the energy in his own body to that of the victim's hand, speeding up the cell reproduction and the rejuvenation process. *Why shouldn't we be able to speed up the reproduction of cells as we have speeded up the way of travel?* Certainly our mind is grand enough to enable us to direct the energy forces within us to do greater things than those we have done with it thus far. Psychic development will light the way to the future. Psychic power can be expected to meet many human and protective needs. This can all be done through well-trained and correctly motivated psychics, basing their ability on God power. At the present time, it is almost impossible for the average person —with or without known psychic ability—to form a clear, precise thought-form, free from emotional distortions. It is because he cannot control his mental images with any degree of success. It is God power that can bring about this change.

It is the power that is yours for the asking.

CHAPTER THREE

When I call the ultimate source of wisdom God power, it is with a deep sense of reverence, for no matter how well we develop our own psychic ability, most of what we like to do we can't do without calling upon the God power of the universe. One of the greatest religious writers of the twentieth century, Ellen G. White, drew the same conclusion.

In *Testimonies*, Volume 3, page 138, she stated: "God endowed man with so great a vital force that he has withstood the accumulation of disease brought upon the race in consequence of perverted habits and has continued for 6,000 years. This fact in itself is enough to evidence to us the *strength and electrical energy that God gave to man at his creation.* . . . *'If Adam at his creation had not been endowed with 20 times as much vital force as men now have, the race with their present habits of living in violation of natural law would have become extinct.'*"

Another one of her statements in *Spiritual Gifts*, Volume 3, page 84, is in accordance with this thought:

"Those who lived before the flood come forth with their

giant height and stature, more than twice as tall as men now living upon the earth and well proportioned," she writes. "The generations after the flood were less in stature." And she goes on to say that the degeneration caused by the fall of man disfigured the human race, both physically and mentally.

Vital force, electrical force, God power—to me they are all synonymous. It is a known principle, but very few ever regard God power as a force that can be used in our daily battle for survival.

To be a psychic is really nothing new—it is merely making use of a force that is as yet not fully understood. I firmly believe that degeneration of the human race caused us to lose one of our basic faculties, that which gave us psychic insight. It is apparent that various members of the animal kingdom have not been affected by this process as severely as we have, and consequently, their psychic power and mental insight is still intact. They are still provided with a degree of intuitive power unknown to us. It is not that animals or even plants were endowed with more of this power than we were, but that they have consistently and continuously used it, through necessity, owing to better means of communication. Fish in the ocean, a mouse in a field, a lonely bird winging its way in search of prey; they all require their psychic power for survival.

I am convinced that as a race we have lost much of what we once possessed. That this degeneration has taken on alarming proportions can be clearly recognized when one realizes that in patriarchal days and in the time of Christ, for example, most of the biblical characters were highly intuitive and "psychic." Scoffers and those proud of their disbelief in psychic phenomena are in for a shock, especially during the coming decade, for extensive scientific research presently being conducted at major universities and research centers throughout the world has established *proof* of the existence of mental communication. An article in *Electronics World* of April, 1970, reveals some pertinent facts with regard to this searching investigation.

"At the research center of Rockland State Hospital, N.Y.," it states, "scientists used instruments linked to a computer to record EEG changes in blood volume, in a finger, and heart rate. The human subjects (in this instance husband and wife) were placed in separate rooms and subjected to emotional stimuli. When, for example, the husband was shown a projected picture of his ex-fiancée, the record of his emotional response was matched on his wife's tracings, even though her projection screen was blank. As Dr. Esser, the principal investigator, points out, only a very few people have this bond. He also reports that alpha waves (brain waves) in identical twins are synchronized. This ties in with the odd observation that twins frequently have an almost identical psychic life."

Dr. G. D. Wasserman, another expert mentioned in the same article, in speaking about the Psi-fields that enable individuals to have paranormal experiences, stated that "these are regarded as having 'very narrowly spaced energy levels' and occupy wide regions of space." Thus, according to Wasserman, Psi-fields emit and receive "extremely small quanta of energy."

And Dr. Wasserman mentions the interesting laboratory work done in relation to these "Psi-fields."

"At the Maimonides Medical Center in Brooklyn, for example," and again I quote the *Electronics World* story, "it appears that its dream laboratory was able to induce mental images telepathically in sleeping persons by an 'agent' located in another room about 100 feet away. The transmitting person, the agent, concentrated on a picture chosen from a group of famous paintings and tried to direct this thought-image at a sleeper. The lab was established in 1962, and according to Drs. M. Ullman and S. Krippner, results have been good."

What can be concluded from all this?

After examining all phases of this psychic research and relating them to the accomplishments of Cleve Backster, who discovered what is now known as the "Backster effect," the magazine determined: *"These and related considerations lead to the idea that psi is but a part of a so-called 'paranormal matrix'—a unique communications grid that binds all life together. Its phenomena apparently work on a multi-input basis which operates beyond the known physical laws."*

Thus even reputable scientists support the concept of inborn human energy being responsible for many of the psychic phenomena that have puzzled men down through the ages. No wonder that researchers, intrigued by these results, are intensely stimulated to probe still deeper into this mystery of the universe.

So psychic force *does* exist, much to the chagrin of the expert skeptics, and one does *not* have to live a perfect Christian life in order to be a psychic. A belief in a Higher Being, however, is essential when it comes to drawing upon the knowledge of a Higher Intellect. Therefore, being psychic in itself does not necessarily mean that you must be some sort of a spiritual giant. You can be psychic but still as fickle and earthy as any human can be.

No matter what some of today's well-known psychics may want you to believe, *being a sensitive does not mean that that particular person is consciously in constant touch—or in fact, in touch at all—with the Holy Spirit.* Certainly there are psychics who have received additional power from a Superior Being, Who is using that person to relay Its will to humanity, but generally a psychic is just someone endowed with more or less of a developed sixth sense and has not become that way because of a privileged connection with a Higher Being.

You are psychic because you're you and for no other reason. The *psychic* power *is* you; it is *within* you; it is your *birthright*—yet one that is seldom claimed. What you do with that birthright is a responsibility you will have to live with for the rest of your life.

Is a psychic necessarily wicked? Does he have to be on the side of Good or Evil? I have asked myself that question numerous times, but once I became cognizant of the *origin* of psychic power, the answer readily presented itself with unmistakable clarity.

It is like finding yourself in a big city library and letting your eyes wander over the thousands of books that line the shelves. Your mind is open; you want to have *something* to read. The choice of subject matter is yours. Do you want something that will elevate your mind and increase your knowledge of the better things of life? Or would you prefer to nourish the lower instincts within you and allow your negative vibrations to get the upper hand? It is your own choice that determines whether you use the accumulated knowledge of good or the tarnished assortment of evil. It is the same way with the psychic. His *ability* can be enlarged, developed and used to draw upon the powers of good or evil, but this choice is left entirely up to him.

Ask yourself these questions before you cross the threshold of the Unknown. "Why do I want this power?" and "What do I want to do with it?"

There are many examples of psychics who, in biblical days, made the wrong choice, tuned into the wrong power line and found evil waiting at the road's end. The Bible speaks of prophets, of holy men of old, and these men were without a doubt on the side of God; however, there were also soothsayers and wizards possessing the *same* inherent power who exploited their power in a degenerate and iniquitous way, and because of this, God recognized them not.

If you have convinced yourself that you desire this ability, then the task of developing the psychic power you already possess comes next—and this is the hard part. *Even* for the trained psychic, it is not always easy to differentiate between a *psychic impression, pure imagination and a revelation of supernatural origin.* This is one of the first requisites, and only rigorous training can help overcome this human handicap. That is why the apprentice psychic makes so many errors. Psychic discernment develops very slowly; it is the most important part of your development. A psychic mind has no problem "seeing" things, and a vast amount of events and happenings crosses its vision. In my life I see incidents and occurrences just as clearly as though they were happening right before my eyes. When I concentrate on a person, it is as if his life rolls off like a documentary, revealing the past, the present and often unavoidable events that are waiting for a mere catalyst to be brought into the "now."

I once walked up to a woman sitting in the audience who had her hands resting in her lap, one hand completely covering the other.

I placed my hand on her shoulder and brought her into psychic view.

"I like that ring of yours," I confided to her, "but I prefer the other one you have, the much larger ring—the one that came to you with lots and lots of love."

Her breath stopped short. She was surprised and startled.

"Yes . . . it did," she whispered slightly alarmed, "but how—"

"It's a beautiful ring," I continued, "the setting is exquisite and unusual. I am sure I would recognize it if I ever saw it—"

"Would you?" she questioned smilingly, looking into my eyes, and with a slow but deliberate movement, she brought her hidden hand into view. On her finger was displayed the ring I had been admiring sight unseen.

This example is typical of a psychic's ability to "see" things not ordinarily visible to others. A psychic can see "through" as well as "beyond." I felt the ring psychically. It becomes a matter of "feeling," of having the psychic's discerning ability to pick out the impression from between the flares of imagination that tend to obscure psychic reality. I can well remember the days when I was desperately trying to learn how to differentiate between fantasy, imagination, impressions, etc. Not a week passes that someone approaches me with one of the questions that also plagued *me* so often in my early days. "I had a dream last night," they say, "and dreamed some horrible things—what do they mean?" And without giving me enough details, they fully expect me to jump up, open the cloak of secrecy and locate their missing dream that meant so little to them that they forgot about it before they even awakened. People like that always make me smile, for Alka-Seltzer is usually all they'd need to solve their problem. What they really meant to say was, "I ate too much last night and had a bad case of indigestion."

I must emphasize, however, that there is only one way in which a person can learn how to "feel" the difference between imagination and a true psychic impression and that is through *practice*. The awareness of my ability came to me at an early age, but it was through continuous practice that I developed it. Years later it paid off handsomely when I began to use it selling organs while working my way through college. Within weeks after hitting the trail—"churching" through the countryside—I became the best organ salesman Old Wiley Lyons ever had, but when I tried to explain my success to him, he just shook his head and grunted.

"Just can the explanation, Dave," he'd grumble indifferently, "just keep on sellin' 'em!"

I recall how one day while driving down a dirt road with Wiley Lyons, I sensed a church some three miles up ahead.

"There's a church coming up, Wiley," I said, "and they need an organ. Let's go and sell 'em."

Wiley just scratched his head and gave me that puzzled grin of his that I'd seen cross his face so often when we happened to be together.

"Go git 'em, boy." He smiled. "I'll watch you."

Within minutes we pulled up in front of a small but dignified-looking church and walked up to the parsonage to see the preacher.

"I am here to sell you a new organ," I said, introducing myself as the purveyor of the world's greatest organs.

The preacher gave me a long and conservative look, probably the one he reserved for slippery southern con men.

"We sure do need a new one, brother," he answered in his most imposing tone of voice, trying not to disagree with me, "but," he continued, "we'll have to wait until Christmas before we can afford it." Having conveyed his message, he gently backed off and started to close the door.

"Oh, no, you don't have to," I broke in, carefully trying to keep him from shutting the door all the way. "Christmas can be as close as you want it to be," and proceeded to explain our liberal trade-in policy to him.

And while a stunned Wiley looked on, I sold the preacher a sizable organ, complete with steeple chimes. He was right though; he didn't get his organ until Christmastime. That year, however, his yuletide holiday was celebrated smack in the middle of July, because that was when I delivered the massive organ, together with a six-foot Christmas tree dressed with the prettiest of trimmings and the brightest of lights!

Was it just good salesmanship that made me a success in the organ business, or was there more to it? I prefer to believe there was.

The apprentice psychic should never disregard a hunch or a strong imaginary impression. Many of them are *real* and not illusory at all, but to the untrained mind they may seem so. Approximately fifty per cent of your imagination is no doubt made up of psychic impressions, but unless you step out and try them or put them to the test of reality, you will never know what you missed.

To reiterate, *everything is contingent on practice for the newborn psychic.* Your mind can be likened to the fingertip of a safecracker. Unless it is sanded down to almost raw nerve, it will not be able to pick up the clicking of the tumblers. The same holds true for your inner mind. Unless it is adequately trained and fine tuned to pick up the vibrations that converge on it from all directions, it will not be able to select the desired frequency, and the impulses that reach it will move in and out without control.

Every psychic makes mistakes. I made (and still make) my share of them. In my early years I would practice my psychic perception by walking up to a person, meditating for a moment while standing close to him, and saying, "Your name is Larry!" I wouldn't ask, I would just blurt it out.

More often than not, I'd be wrong, and the person would immediately correct me.

"No, it's Harry."

I would apologize and then continue just the same with different people and different questions, day after day, until several weeks had passed, and I noticed that my average of hits had increased remarkably, and I was quite close to getting a perfect score. It was then that I expanded my scope and began using the telephone. On many occasions people will call me and ask for help regarding their specific problem. Invariably my reply is to have them concentrate on themselves.

"Think of yourself, blotting out every other impression or thought," I tell them. "Only when you do this am I able to concentrate on you and intercept your channel—your wave length. *Think of yourself and then consciously think of your own private communications channel.*" I explain this to them not because it helps *me*, but because it will aid *them* in understanding how I operate. Once they concentrate on themselves, I can break in and tune in to their private channel in much the same way as a variable condenser enables us to tune our radio to a specific station. You may be inclined to think that inasmuch as this contact involves real thought power—real energy—it will be easier to pick up the channel of someone calling from the same city or in the immediate area than that of a man or woman calling from a distance of approximately two thousand miles, but this is not so. It is just the other way around, owing to the human element that enters the picture. The fact is that someone who calls from nearby usually doesn't try as hard to concentrate as the person who is calling from a considerable distance, because his phone call will cost half as much. Consequently, his conversation may not be as intense as the man who wants real help for his money.

Even in my telephone work, I began with the hits outnumbered by the misses. Frequently the flares of information that spring at me while the caller is fixing his thoughts on himself are incomplete because of his own confused thought patterns. Therefore, when I would receive the impression of a small animal in his or her vicinity, I'd say, "I see a little animal close to you," not being at all sure whether it was a cat or a dog, but relying on the person to interrupt and confirm, "Yes, I have a cat," or, "Do you mean my dog?" It was in this manner that my ability was helped along, until I finally began to recognize certain vibrations belonging to specific animals, taking practically all the guesswork out of it.

I could have started by asking, "Is that a dog I see at your feet?" but if I were mistaken, the faith and confidence that they had in me might be destroyed. I was aware from the beginning that my thinking had to be positive. It nourished my enthusiasm and strengthened their faith in my ability to help them. Making a positive statement is like beaming positive power to a person. This is really what people mean when they say they are encouraging someone to do something. They are actually sending out beams of positive force, strengthening the receiver's already existing ability to do something.

In some ways these beams can be compared to radar, for not only do they go out to strengthen, but they can also be sent out expressly to track down and retrieve information. It is the property of these rays that enables me (and others) to make predictions, although not every psychic or clairvoyant will concede to this fact. Many of them, while preparing to make a prediction or when realizing that they will be called upon to make a profound announcement of inspiration, will take several days to concentrate on the subject at hand, concluding their mental vigil with a long-expected prediction. I work altogether differently. My most meaningful predictions have come when I started speaking with the *intent* to predict or the *intent* to inform. Seldom am I aware of what I am going to forecast when "relaying" retrieved information, and I have good reasons for not studying and making ready my predictions beforehand. I recall numerous times when I would concentrate on important topics in the news or on the problems of the cities where I was scheduled to speak, but if it ever worked—and thinking back now, I am doubtful—it surely came to an abrupt end on January 2, 1967, when I spoke at the downtown Optimist Club in Memphis, Tennessee. It was one of those events where I felt that I had better make preparations so as not to commit a serious blunder, and at four o'clock in the afternoon on the preceding day, I sat down at my typewriter, concentrated deeply and wrote down my predictions. I listed them in precisely the same way as I was going to deliver them, and once written I put them away until the following morning. But that day the most amazing thing happened! More than half of them had already been fulfilled by the time I had reached the Optimist Club.

"These happenings are headlined in today's paper," someone shouted, interrupting my lecture, "that's old news." One quick glance at the morning's paper confirmed my feeling that something had indeed gone wrong. No matter what I managed to say in front of that skeptical audience that day, nothing would convince them I was sincere. I knew what had happened, and I could accept the facts. It was a typical case of drawing information from the universal knowledge that surrounds us. I had picked up existing vibrations of what had and still was actually taking place at that very moment. Waves of information had reached me while the events were in the making, but not realizing this, I had regarded them as predictions and made myself look like a fool at a meeting where I was to speak on the ability of the psychic to foresee the future. What a psychic! What a future! Needless to say I never again worked my predictions a day in advance.

Understanding now that I can draw upon the vibrations around us at any time and on any occasion, I leave this "homework" alone and rely on the impulses that reach me at the moment when I need them, unless of course, they are of a long-range nature. These forecasts, however, can safely be made because of the time element involved. On the other hand, the danger with these forecasts lies in the fact that many pseudo-psychics become too deeply involved with them, relying on the possibility that as long as they make them fifty or sixty years in advance, no one alive today will be able to attack their credibility.

Even though many psychics make a scrutinizing study of what they intend to predict (very rarely are predictions made spontaneously), I arrive at them through a process of mental concentration and attain the desired results within a matter of minutes, sometimes seconds. Those who have observed me in concentration relate that as soon as I go into this deep state of mental alertness, my entire body seems to become tense, my eyes begin to squint and my facial expression changes. I don't see these changes, but to me what I feel is much more meaningful. Within seconds after my decision to concentrate, all of my senses seem to become highly intensified. Just the faintest whiff of perfume on a woman seated in the last row of the auditorium to me begins to smell like the sweet fragrance of a field of flowers permeating the air, the slightest touch becomes a painful experience and the prevailing light in the room works on my eyes like a powerful beacon trying to reach into my inner soul. I concentrate and force myself to go deeper and deeper and probe still further into the unknown until I reach the ability to penetrate the channels of communication that exist for every one of us—and then BOOM! I am there. It has happened. My mind ceases to concentrate, and a peaceful feeling invades my body. The next thing I know is that events are rolling off before my eyes and painful reality consumes me.

A classic example of this was the prediction I made about hurricane Camille. Before appearing on television one evening, I dashed off some hasty notes dealing with various subjects I wanted to cover; yet as I started to speak, my mind was suddenly flooded with impressions almost too horrible to repeat. In rapid succession, flashes of predictions concerning the tragedy of hurricane Camille shot through me like lightning.

Another image that will always be branded in my mind is one I saw while foretelling a tragic automobile accident on a bridge, the badly torn body of the driver lying on the rocks below. I conveyed my gory impressions to the audience and stated that the victim would be identified by his plaid clothing. Six months later the accident occurred. A car passing through town skidded out of control while on the bridge. The driver was thrown clear of the car and over the railing of the bridge, falling to his death on the rocks. Witnesses said they were reminded of my forecast when they realized the victim was wearing plaid clothing. . . .

How could I project that accident so far in advance? How was I able to see minor details such as the plaid clothing? I have long ceased to be shocked by these precise forebodings. It strengthens my conviction that in time and space, in the realm of the sixth dimension, there is no future and no past, and everything seems to happen in the "now." Psychic research, still in its infancy, has such vast unexplored areas that we will encounter more questions as new facts become known to us. There are as yet no absolute experts in the field of psychic research, and no man has come up with satisfactory explanations. A true psychic is one who has learned how to trigger the latent power of the mind, and there is no doubt that eventually man will find himself back on the ladder of mental progress from which he has fallen through inbreeding and degeneration.

The emphasis on psychic phenomena of the last few years has caused much confusion and distortion of some very basic issues. Relying as I do on the inborn power of every human being, I am vehemently opposed to so-called "spirit control," communication with "departed entities" or the idea that every psychic happening is the result of intervention by a supernatural being. Once you are on your way and develop your own power, you will be able to make profound psychic predictions within a short period of time and tap the cosmic resource. But—and this is most important— the ability to distinguish between a psychic impression and interference in human affairs by a power of the sixth dimension has to be developed. You can be psychic without having supernatural powers enter your life, but only when you recognize the difference will you be able to know the value of what you receive.

I have often been asked whether I go into a trance and am controlled by a spirit when I make my predictions. *Nothing is further from the truth.* One need not go into a trance to reach one's inner power, and, as previously mentioned, psychic power has nothing to do with spirit control. My intense concentration is usually of short duration, but it is so deep and so total that I am completely withdrawn, and my surroundings are absolutely obscured from me. The difference between what I do and going into a trance is that my method allows me to utilize my psychic ability. A trance, on the other hand, is a method under which another power possesses the mind of the medium, depriving him of all personal control. There have been situations where outsiders may have gotten the idea that certain information I sought came to me from supernatural agents, as when a hyperdistressed woman came to me to discover where her father had deposited his will.

"If we can't find it," she said nervously, "we will be in real trouble."

It took me just a few moments of intense concentration

to give her the address of the bank, the name of the bank manager and the number of his safe-deposit box.

"Better go right now," I advised her, "and hurry, for the banker isn't even aware that your father's dead, and this will make it easier for you to gain access to the box."

Now, what occurred here? Some people might think that I gained this information from a supernatural source. A medium might say, "Your father appeared to me and told me such and such . . ." He also might claim direct communication with the "spirit" of the departed, trying to make it sound more mysterious than it really is. I didn't hear any voices; there were no Unknown Visitors that approached me and showed or disclosed the required information. I believe that when a person dies, his last thoughts—his conscious vibrations—still linger on. They vibrate on their own "assigned" frequency, and my concentration enabled me to locate that frequency and tap it. All I did was track down the frequency path the man had established in his life and eavesdrop.

Inconceivable? Frequencies continue whether we prefer it or not. A number of years ago, a television viewer in England stared with incredulity when he suddenly saw the call letters of a Houston, Texas, TV station appear on his screen. Astounded by such transmitting power, the viewer called Houston information and requested the phone number of the station.

"Sorry, sir," came back the polite reply of the operator, "that station went off the air three years ago."

Further checking revealed that it had indeed gone off the air at the time the operator said it had. The signal received by the British viewer was part of a program broadcast by the station shortly before it ceased operating; however, owing to a freak of nature, it was intercepted in space by a distant star and bounced back to earth to be seen by the alert

Englishman. *It had been on the way for three long years.* The signal arrived and was recognized, but the source had already ceased to exist. The same principle applies to the stars that we "see." Just because we receive the light does not mean that the star that transmitted the light is still in existence. Once a signal has been broadcast, it continues to exist and to travel independently from its source.

These are the signals that surround us. The only thing that makes a psychic different from the people around him is that he has learned to tune in to these signals. Accomplishing this is a skill that must be developed through extensive and specific training to be discussed more fully in the following chapters. Training will help you distinguish between pure fantasy, psychic impressions and intervention by the supernatural; but it is the psychic impressions that concern us most of all, for they form the basis of our ability. Sensitives have a tendency to regard ordinary impulses as manifestations of the supernatural, but they forget that even the prophets of old did not live within a chain reaction of revelations. Supernatural revelations cannot be classified as commonplace occurrences. They are rare and are usually the result of God's desire to reveal His will to man, often completely disregarding His subject's preparedness. To say that every psychic impulse is emitted by the Holy Spirit is nothing short of blasphemy. People who acknowledge Satan's control over their destinies are unique; when calamities transpire in their lives or something outstanding happens to them, they usually blame or thank the Holy Spirit. If a catastrophe strikes, they call it God's will or say it was "meant this way," yet the Lord may not have had anything to do with it. It may simply have been the result of the law of cause and effect. But what sounds more elevating than crediting it to the Holy Spirit? Incorporating Him into their experience makes it appear that they are a part of God's "inner circle" of confidants, and to create this impression they will do just about anything.

There is a place for the action of the Holy Spirit in our lives, but it is not up to the psychics to decide where and when that should be. The Holy Spirit is a part of what I know as God force or God power. The more you become aware of your own power, the more you will become aware of your limitations and of the important and vital role in your life reserved for God power.

CHAPTER FOUR

Scientists tell us that we use approximately one-tenth of our brain. It is a startling observation, for if that one-tenth is responsible for everything from safety pins to hydrogen bombs, then it is rather frightening to imagine what our capabilities might be if we were able to employ the power of our *entire* brain. With our one-tenth, we are discovering ways to reach the outer rim of the known solar system, and that same one-tenth created the *beep—beep* of the first Sputnik and introduced us to the heart-shaking roar of the mighty Saturn rockets that put our first men on the moon. While some heroes comb the vastness of space, others drift into the treacherous depths of the oceans searching for earth's hidden treasures. Man reaches outward to find himself, neglecting to reach inward first to explore the possibilities of the unused nine-tenths of his brain. If used properly, it can give him access to knowledge never before revealed, making it unnecessary to travel outward to discover the clues of his very existence in all their nakedness.

You do not have to be a mental giant to realize that if a mere one-tenth of our brain is responsible for all our accomplishments thus far, the remaining nine-tenths must be able to contribute considerably more. But to say that the "neglected" segment of the human brain is the part that is accountable for psychic feelings and unexplained supernatural phenomena is something that no one as yet can ascertain. I am convinced and this conviction is upheld by modern research—that it is the *entire* being that is psychic. Psychic ability is not limited only to the sensitivity of the brain; our whole self "perceives." The nervous system is responsible for much more than we give it credit for. It assists us in tuning in to long-lost powers. Not so long ago, Russian scientists reported that several people had proven their ability to recognize colors by *touch* under strict scientific supervision. Our body senses these things—not our brain. Each living cell seems to be able to act as an independent intelligent agency, and together they form the "psychic recognition system"—the PRS—that is part of every living being.

The question of how to awaken and how to alert this system is therefore of extreme importance if you want to live as a whole human being.

As I was sitting in my office some years ago wondering how to help those who came day after day seeking guidance, the answer came to me. My theological background may have had a decided influence upon the formulation of my four power-steps. Formulating them helped me; explaining them to others helps them. Here are the steps:

(1) *Desire it*

That this is a basic step should be clear to everyone, seeker or nonseeker. Before you can do anything or acquire anything, you have to desire it. It is the emotion that triggers the Law of Cause and Effect and propels your obvious as well as your hidden talents into motion.

Let us take a modern example and trace it all the way through our four steps and see how it works. Our example is a young boy of nineteen with the fanatical desire to be an astronaut and travel the outlying reaches of the universe. He wants to be admired. The desire to "be" has become a phobia, and he sets the steps in motion. Wanting to become one of the "new" generation, he begins to associate with others striving for the same goal and starts to exchange information, sharing his dreams and strengthening his ambition. His surroundings secure, he automatically enters a new phase of his career. He is reaching for the second step on the ladder. His desire has fully awakened him. Now it is time to act.

(2) Seek after it

Being completely aware of the line his life should follow from now on, he endeavors to investigate the best schools, ponders which courses to take and broadens his contacts, hoping for the right person who can put him on the trail of a scholarship. He is now beginning to shape his future course of action, and with his basic desire strengthened with the possibility of success, he begins to act like a bulldog, heading for the ultimate goal, no matter what the cost. He now not only enrolls in the best school available, but also sets forth to utilize all his spare time, filling in the little gaps of his vast knowledge so that he can become *the best*, not just *one* of the best. Competition is fierce, and every college course becomes a challenge, a hurdle that has to be surmounted. Now he again seeks others with the same interests, but this time it is not to compare techniques or desires, it is to broaden his horizon and expand his contacts so he knows where to go and whom to use when the training is finished.

(3) *Accept it*

Training accomplished, mission is now ahead. Recognizing fully the road to take and which contacts to use, he now sets out to accept the practical positions that will line him up for the big one. No job is too small, no challenge too great. The Cosmos is just round the bend, and this is the screening process that will terminate with the final selection of the newest member of the team. Now he is no longer afraid. He knows his knowledge is superior to that of the other candidates, for he has diligently followed each logical step subconsciously outlined for him. With faith in his ability, he faces the board, and subsequently, he finds himself leaving the room a new astronaut, prepared for action.

(4) *Use it*

Using it has now become the end of the road, but unknown to him, the same four steps begin to operate all over again. To stay on top, he must have the desire to remain there. Subconsciously he aspires to make this possible, and once arrived, he accepts the reality of higher rank and elevated social standing, followed by the responsibility it entails. He is now caught in the proverbial vicious circle, only this one ends in an outward spiral, enlarged both in scope and size each time a new desire enters his life.

The plan outlined here may appear too simple to be acceptable to you, yet world empires have been built on these points. Perhaps, if you are religiously inclined, you may want to use these steps to guide you into God's Plan of Salvation. Here too, it works, for psychic development is built on biblical principles. This is only natural, since it was God who installed the seeds of all our abilities within us. Christ Himself introduced these principles into the world when He walked among us.

These points are not just applicable to mental and spiritual development, but as outlined in the example, they are also infinitely practical in daily affairs. As soon as you begin to apply the steps to your psychic development, you start flexing your imagination, visualizing yourself in desirable situations and enviable circumstances. You begin to *imagine* consciously, looking for ways to increase the beauty and value of your illusory situation until it almost becomes real. It is here that you are reaching deep within you, for imagination is the lowest form of psychic ability. Once this is recognized and accepted, you can *force* these fanciful situations into reality by concentrating on them and making every one of your actions a thread in the grand design.

The four-step method is the basic guide and will enable you to unfold the power you seek. The moment you start using it, you begin to tap the resources within you. This, however, and keep this in mind, is *not* the same as acquiring the ability to tap the power of the Sixth Dimension. Only when you have prepared yourself by having sharpened your psychic being can you expand into the Unmeasurable.

How many dimensions are there? you ask. Really, no one knows. There may be many worlds in many dimensions existing simultaneously around us and through us. They may be occupying the same space and time as we are; but they are nevertheless invisible to us, for we are physical beings with physical functions, locked by necessity in a physical world.

The first way to expand your psychic birthright is—and I cannot emphasize this enough—strict adherence to the four-step method. It is the most logical way to mental expansion, for it uses Godly principles to tap a God-given power or rejuvenate a God-given talent.

Daily Exercises Accompanying the Four-Step Method

Constant practice of proven ways to sharpen your "mind-vision" is a must if you want to succeed in making the four-step method work for you.

Those who proudly profess to be agnostics will no doubt frown when I draw once more upon the Bible to prime the psychic pump. It is there, imprisoned in the majesty and beauty of the 91st Psalm and the Lord's Prayer, that we find the material we need. Both of these have a meaning that far exceeds our limited awareness, and I use them and claim their promised power. To me being a psychic is more listening to a calling than working at a profession. It has become my life's work. However, I would not be able to maintain a constant mental vigil were it not for the fact that I can draw upon a Power higher than myself. My regular devotional period is the key to power for the day. This contact should be and *can* be yours if you believe.

You may regard this as the primary exercise that will be your guide until your last day on earth.

On the more "practical" side, there are many mental training fragments—together making up the "Book of Mental Expansion"—that you should make your own.

One of my early exercises was more a memory sharpener than anything else. A friend of mine had a house tucked away deep in the northern Maine woods, and since I had been there only on one occasion, it required intense concentration to remember everything about it. So, sitting down in a straight-backed chair, eyes closed and feeling completely at ease, I'd try to let my mind wander back to that house. I would envision myself observing the house from a great height—viewing the surrounding landscape, trees, gentle brook, mass of green foliage—and slowly I would descend lower and lower until each tree became a separate entity and I was able to count the shingles on the roof. Like a zoom lens I would move in closer and closer until I began to smell the freshly mowed grass in the front yard and could see the bees darting from blossom to blossom. A second later I'd feel my feet touch the ground, and straightening my clothes, I'd start to walk around the house, noticing the coiled garden hose and the rusty old pan half-hidden in the muddy puddle beside the back entrance. I'd try the front door and find it locked most of the time. Invariably, I'd saunter around to the back, push down the door handle and walk in—and from that moment on, I'd be in the hands of my memory. At first it was difficult to remember even one thing about it, although the more I tried, the more I would recall items that I know now I saw during that one and only visit, yet whose image had completely slipped my mind. I would then walk from room to room, starting in the kitchen, being very aware of everything surrounding me, including the yellow harvest pans, the towel hanging on that one lonely nail and that spot of grease on the electric toaster sitting in the corner of the breakfast nook. I would even notice the crumbs of whole wheat bread on the floor near the table leg. I'd look at the door handles, the flaking paint. Occasionally I'd find myself opening a cupboard and taking out a cup to examine it closely. The same old cracks were still on the enamel surface, and that age-old tea stain still hadn't been washed off.

I would leave the kitchen and wander around the living room, fingering the green velvet drapes, blowing off an occasional bit of dust. The softness of the wall-to-wall carpeting always impressed me as I moved from room to room, and even the faded prints on the hallway wall made me nostalgic, for they were so similar to the ones we had in our home when I was a child.

Day after day I experienced trips similar to this one, imagining myself in many different places where I had been over the years until I ultimately felt that I didn't need my imagination any longer. I then began to visualize places where I was certain I had never been but always yearned to be. I would lie down at night with the idea of sleeping, but before drifting off, I would take trips and would picture things so distinctly that it no longer seemed like fantasy. It became reality.

I was there, I believed, but the tiniest speck of doubt still lingered until an insurance man hearing of my interest came to see me and questioned me regarding my research into the psychic world. His queries reflected his complete sincerity, and eager to please him, I decided to provide him with an example of the limitless possibilities of psychic power. I picked up a piece of paper and started to sketch the ground plan of his home and then proceeded to describe his house in its entirety, the way I did my mental exercises, realizing of course that I had never been in his house. I identified every room and named each item and its location. Affirmatively he continued to nod his head. In the living room I veered abruptly and walked through an open door into the bedroom. There I stopped.

"Oh-oh, I'd better quit here," I remarked candidly. "Your wife's here. She is straightening out the bedroom," and I went on to describe her to the minutest detail.

"That *has* to be her," he answered, somewhat startled by this sudden turn in my imaginative journey, "only *she* looks that way at this time of day."

Three hours after he left the phone rang. It was my insurance visitor. He was on the verge of having a nervous breakdown and was so agitated he could barely converse understandably.

"David, I have to tell you this," he stammered. "Let me tell you what happened. I got home and found my wife in a complete state of shock. She was crying uncontrollably.

'Someone was with me in the house today,' she sobbed hysterically, 'and I couldn't see him! I was working around the house,' she went on, 'and suddenly someone was following me from room to room. I could feel him come in and stop while I was making the beds. It scared me half to death!'

"I told her then about our meeting today, and when we compared notes, we both realized that my wife's visitor had been in the house at exactly the same time as you were describing the place to me.

"It was no mere coincidence," he shouted, obviously shaken. "You were there David, you were there!"

Experiences such as this are the logical outcome of a life of almost unending mental exercises. From the moment you get up in the morning, you should live your day according to a preset pattern. You should start by not only perceiving the problems ahead but also sensing the solutions to those problems. You must force yourself to become one with the problem. If you succeed, you will find intuitive solutions to the problems you are facing or will discover ways to attain the same goal. You should live in a constant air of perception, of intuition, for this will enable you to open yourself up to the workings of your inner mind.

Since developing your psychic self is closely connected with the growth of your self-confidence, *the elimination of fear in any form should be one of your major objectives.* When we speak of fear, we have in mind an emotion we share with our fellow human beings, yet it is not natural for us to fear. It is acquired, and yet it is difficult if not impossible for anyone to remember the time when fear was not in the air. However, we can form a habit of conquering it in much the same manner as we have formed it. Getting rid of fear boils down to adopting the right attitude. It means having self-confidence and this can only be obtained through faith in the God power of the universe. The philosophy underlying the eradication of fear is simple, and again, this too has God as its basis.

Learning how to love is the first step in the elimination of fear. In 1 John 4:18 it states that "Perfect love casteth out all fear," so you cannot experience the emotions of love and fear simultaneously. You cannot *resent* and love at the same time; you cannot *hate* and love at the same time; and you cannot *fear* and love at the same time. Living without fear signifies that you have mastered the art of living with respect, trust, faith and love.

There are six important steps you must follow if you wish to overcome your fear. Practice each step three minutes per day for ten days. Your entire outlook will change, and fear will be eradicated from your life.

(1) *Read the 91st Psalm.*

Read it with intent to learn; read it with the will to learn. Its sixteen verses contain no less than twenty-eight Godly promises, each one enabling you to gain trust and develop faith—elements essential to triumphing over fear.

(2) *Spend three minutes thinking about all the things you love about yourself.*

This is to help you realize that you have unique qualities, possibly far superior to those of the people around you. You are an individual, specially created, and the rare combination of qualities for which you are known makes you unique. There is no one like you, and you have a reason to be proud of yourself and your accomplishments, no matter how small. Love yourself because you're you, if for no other reason. List all the points you admire in yourself and the ones you feel others should admire in you. It is your first step to gaining self-confidence.

(3) *The next three minutes should be spent recounting all the good things that happened to you yesterday.*

Let's face it, no matter how bad things seem, something good must have happened to you yesterday. Try to relive each hour of the day; force yourself to remember what you did from hour to hour and enumerate the things that did work out your way "in spite of," or that happened your way because you fought for them. You never know how many good things happened to you until you count and list them. Look at them. They are important, for they can show you what you can really do, while you weren't even really trying.

(4) *Following these three minutes, you want to spend three thinking of someone you resent and send them love.*

That should be the easiest of all. We all have people we resent or are jealous of or just plain hate. To bring them to mind should be simple. The second part of this point may be more difficult, for it is contrary to human nature to send love to those we hate or to those who hate us. We know that love is a force and that the vibrations of love can be beamed to those individuals we select as our targets, so be conscious of this as you direct your thought power. Think of that person and tell yourself, "I'd love to help you, I'd love to be with you," or similar forced thoughts. Concentrate on that person and try to imagine your love beams leaving you and traversing the miles and touching the one you are trying to influence. It will reach him and influence him *if you wish it to happen.* At the same time it will change your resentment or hatred into tolerance and transform it from tolerance into love. It is through your desire to help them that you help yourself, and by enlarging the element of love in your life, you begin to decrease the power and effects of fear.

(5) *Send love to someone who is sick or may need your love.*

Again, this point is designed to make you less selfish and place you more in harmony with the power of the universe. Everyone we know needs love, but the ones who are ill or in despair require a larger share of it. Search out the one you feel falls in this category and send him your beams of love. Concentrate on him for the full three minutes; think of him, imagine your love reaching him in the form of energy beams and your guiding them to soften his heart, making him more receptive to love and diminishing his needs, whatever they may be.

(6) *Spend three minutes imagining everything you want to have or want to be.*

Is this not selfishness, you may wonder? I don't believe it is. Because you are developing a sincere love in your heart for others and are appreciative of all the good things that have happened to you and have recognized your own abilities, it does not imply that you do not wish your own life to be full and enriched. You are on the way to becoming a part of that love which you have beamed to others and are replacing fear with love. By reason of this, your innermost desires will have a tendency to come true, for now all good things are attracted to you.

Eliminating fear is essential if you wish to advance, yet the six points listed above are only a relatively small step on the road to perfection. It lays the groundwork for what is to follow; it sets the stage on which imagination plays and shows its capabilities. Even if you should proceed no further than the four-step method and the program to dispose of fear in your planned development, you will already have reached a high level of success and attainment, creating in you a feeling of harmony and perfection you never before thought possible.

You are now on the road, but much remains to be accomplished before you will recognize the actual emergence of the "psychic you." If you're satisfied with your development to date after using the four-step method as a basis, then leave the following chapter alone. Forget it, for it is reserved for only those who are deeply and resolutely committed.

CHAPTER FIVE

In the course of teaching psychic development, I invariably utilize a program of Seventeen Power Steps. Before I present them, however, I feel I must answer a question so many of my students ask at this point.

"Why study the Seventeen Steps," they ask, "if we're *not* psychic? Is everyone *really* psychic, as you claim? Can you test us?" and this, frankly, is where I fall apart. The public seems to want a jack-in-the-box method that will give them all the answers to all their questions. They want tests. Tests that will separate the promising psychics from the psychic dropouts. Somewhat like a magic formula that will save a marriage. Let me ask a question in return—*how do you save a marriage?* How? Surely you realize there are many ways to save a marriage, but they all boil down to the fact that you have to work at it. There *are* no magic formulas; no magic tests, no magic remedies that will provide all the answers. Trying to cook up a series of foolproof examinations to test the psychic is even more difficult. For thousands of years now psychic impressions have been forcing their electric currents into the human brain, and ever since that first impression people have tried to devise methods aimed at identifying psychics. What they really have attempted to do is to test the invisible and intangible by physical means. We are not dealing with something that can be explained by a mere mathematical equation—and this very fact is what causes all the inconsistencies in the "experts'" testing methods.

In 1964, my ability as a psychic was questioned by Dr. J. B. Rhine, the famous psychic researcher of Duke University. He exposed me to a number of tests using his now famous psychic cards, but even though I seriously tried to play the game (and it's no more than that) according to his rules, I flunked out. His "tests" indicated that the subject (me) had no psychic ability whatsoever!

Some years previous to that I was at Memphis State University, taking an exam that consisted of twenty-six true-and-false questions. I hadn't studied the subject, nor looked at the questions. I merely covered them with my hand and went down the list, marking the true-and-false boxes the way I felt impelled to. *I got twenty-four out of the twenty-six right*. That was certainly beyond the realm of probability. It can be classified as a psychic phenomena. But, you ask, how did I do it? *I don't know!* I have never yet encountered a method that can effectively test a psychic, and if a psychic can't do this, then how serious and reliable can tests be that are devised by those experts who aren't even psychic themselves?

Testing the psychic is a question that keeps coming up with unceasing persistency, and I have discussed it with many psychologists and psychiatrists who are interested in the psychic world and who use its phenomena in their profession, but even they don't know. Dr. Joe Cassius, psychologist, formerly with the Veterans Hospital in Memphis, Tennessee, and Dr. David Kupfer, a very gifted man who studied with Sigmund Freud, both admitted to me that to their knowledge there is no possible way in which psychic ability in humans can be tested.

One of the main reasons no accurate tests can be devised is that the psychic dimension covers many different facets, each one being responsible for a different manifestation of the psychic world and each one dealing with an entirely different area. *Every person is psychic,* but this does not necessarily mean that they are all psychic in the same way. It stands to reason, therefore, that a standardized test that covers all psychic areas is out of the question. The psychic world is like a vast ocean where each wave represents a different manifestation of the ocean's power. No one device can measure the size of the ocean or the intensity and size of every wave. Even though experienced surfers ride the breakers that hit the South Sea beaches, they know that every ride is a new experience. No two breakers are ever alike.

Take another example. Take twenty professional gamblers and test them with any one of the psychic tests outlined in various folders and leaflets, and they will each produce a different result. *Yet these people are all psychic to a certain extent in the very same field!* And even *here* the tests fail.

It leads to the simple conclusion that testing the psychic is in reality a parlor game and nothing else. Tests are popular. They are intended to show us that we "belong," that we "conform" to the norm. This is the way our life has been regulated, and these self-imposed standards are part of our everyday way of life.

You don't need a test to convince yourself that you're psychic. You have experienced manifestations of this power many times in your own life. Remember the phone call that you felt was coming—and it did? Remember that feeling of uneasiness just before an accident or tragedy? Remember the premonition about a loved one's death? And how about those intuitive feelings about people and places? Look deep into yourself and examine your emotions. Separate fact from fiction, emotional response from premonition, and you too will realize that much of your life is based on *feeling, premonition, intuition, unexplained expectation, and hope. These are the tests that will tell you that you're psychic*—for this is what this book is all about. YOU ARE PSYCHIC—and if you've never experienced the inner voice of your subconscious, you're simply not alive.

So accept the fact that you *are* alive, and that you *are* psychic, and because of your human desire to develop your *entire* being, not just the physical part, you are now ready to embark on the road to the Seventeen Steps.

I have called this course by this name because it takes seventeen steps to reach the second floor of my Memphis home where I have an Upper Room, a serene, tranquil place which I have used for meditation and prayer for many years. To me, my Upper Room is symbolic of the upper room of the mind; a place where we can, perhaps for the first time, meet our inner selves. Yet there is still another reason for the existence of the Upper Room and for my conviction that development of the inherent psychic power is not only desirable, but necessary, if we are to survive this hostile environment.

Throughout the years, I have become increasingly aware of the approach of a terrifying climax to the affairs of human history, events that will engulf the entire human race, partly as the result of humanity's inability to control its own actions, thereby causing the merciless law of cause and effect to be forced into motion. I have tried to condition myself to this frightening knowledge that has become mine. How are you going to tell a mother her son is about to die in Vietnam? How are you going to tell a businessman-friend that he will be completely bankrupt within three weeks? How are you going to tell a wife that her husband has a mistress? I have even seen people plotting other's deaths, and, indeed, seen them carried out the way I sensed it. I have known when a person would be killed in an accident yet was powerless to intervene, as they had set the course of their life toward eternal destruction.

When I started to develop my power, I made serious mistakes. Proud of my new power, I once asked a friend of mine about his father. "How's he doing?" I asked. "Fine," was the answer. "Better than ever before." This should have been my clue to stop, but pride forced me on. "That's what *you* think, Raymond," I replied solemnly. "By Thursday he'll be dead of a heart attack, and you'll be going to his funeral at two thirty this coming Saturday afternoon."

He shrugged it off and drove home and seemingly forgot about my prediction until his father died. Needless to say it was the end of our friendship.

When I first began to use my psychic gift professionally, I soon found the results very depressing and disturbing. Being a psychic carries with it many responsibilities most people are not ready to face or handle. Those who are envious of the "insight" of a psychic should first ask themselves whether they feel ready to accept the horror that often accompanies this vision. If you're born psychic and grow up with the awareness of the invisible world around you, your life becomes one long conditioning process; but to attempt to break through the barrier by pure willpower and without adequate mental preparation can be such a shock that it can even lead to mental breakdown. You have to handle your new gift with respect and caution.

During recent years, awesome predictions of a calamitous nature have been bombarding me with ever-increasing frequency and, during the same time, scores of people have rung my doorbell asking for help. Coincidence? I don't believe so. I feel these people are exposed to the same impulses that reach me, but are unprepared psychically, and it causes deep emotional disturbances within them. They report "danger impulses" and impressions of "unavoidable tragedy." It is, perhaps, the outer fringes of dramatic future events that I sense that have also permeated the subconscious minds of these sensitives. It is for them that I have formulated my Seventeen Steps. They are designed to lead to development and understanding. I join with these sensitives in quiet meditation in the Upper Room.

The Bible says that Jesus went up to the "upper room" and meditated. The apostles, too, went to an "upper room" to receive their instructions after Christ had returned to His Father. Our weakness of character and relaxed determination becomes quite evident when we realize that the apostles remained in their "upper room" for as many as ten or eleven days before the Power came to them, yet we complain that we have meditated an eternity after concentrating a short ten minutes. The apostles went to the Upper Room for a purpose; they had assembled there to receive the Power. There was, however, a purification process that they had to experience, and this was God's reason for postponing the outpouring of His Power. Likened to an old violin, they had to be repaired and tuned by the Master to be ready for their greatest hour, to be in one accord, without resentments or any other dissension. Once they were transmitting love and understanding toward one another, the combined energy force that prevailed within the room put them in harmony with the Power and enabled them to receive.

The walls of Jericho stood and were impregnable until the Israelites marched around them united with one aim—one purpose, and as one, they meditated; and God's Power pulled down the walls.

Silent meditation opens the way to a force that charges you to accomplish the otherwise unreachable.

Inasmuch as the Seventeen Power Steps deal with direct meditation, they do not take the place of the four steps previously outlined. Do not attempt to substitute the seventeen for the four. The four steps are an introduction to the opening of the mind, enabling you to receive the blessings that will become yours through a dedicated use of the seventeen. The four show you the principles and the general outline. The seventeen put them into motion.

Let us now delve into the limitless realm of the Upper Room. Join me, take an easy chair and relax, for you are now ready for the great adventure.

You have no doubt selected a room situated in a quiet section of your house and have shut the windows and pulled the shades. All is peaceful now, and your eyes slowly close. Your conscious thoughts begin to concentrate on your body and tell it to relax. You direct your thoughts until your will is in control of your entire physical being.

Forehead . . . relax!

Ears . . . relax!

Shoulders . . . relax!

Legs . . . relax!

Chest area . . . relax!

Stomach . . . relax!

Muscles . . . relax!

Arms . . . relax!

Think of every part of your body and "tell" it to relax and become completely and unreservedly subject to your will. Prepare yourself for meditation through relaxation and enter the Upper Room in a state of receptiveness.

Now I want you to direct your mind to come with me to the Upper Room; come with me to *your* Upper Room—the Upper Room of your mind, your heart, the secret room where the Power awaits you.

There are Seventeen Steps to the Upper Room, and when you have ascended the last one, you will receive power, you will receive serenity, you will receive ability, for those are all part of the reward. In your Upper Room, you will enter into a new awareness of things your mind never before comprehended. Be relaxed, be ready, for the Upper Room awaits you.

We are ready now. I invite you to place your foot on the first step. Will you walk with me?

ONE   All fear is leaving you now. Think of love, concentrate on love, on the majesty of love, on the *power* of love. Let it enter your soul as it never has before, and you will feel forced to love even your enemies and those who repel you. Love *consumes* you and fear fades out. You are now prepared to move to the next step.

TWO   All resentment leaves you when you direct your mind to move to the second step of this spiritual stairway. Resentment is fading fast because love still consumes you. You no longer resent anyone—person or situation. You are free of resentment; you are becoming a new person.

THREE   This is the step that obliterates all hatred. Hate is one of the ugliest forces to plague mankind. It does not hurt the person to whom it is directed but lowers the vibrations of the hater and places him on an evil plain. Leave it alone! Release it! Let it go! It does not belong in your new life.

FOUR   Hatred is gone, resentment is gone, consuming love is fiercely burning within you, and now is the time to forget all disappointments that have crept into your life. No longer will you have time to dream and nourish thoughts of that which failed. Disappointments are gone now. Things have changed. Your new "you" can no longer be disappointed, for your Love understands all.

FIVE Your new life has no place for jealousies, and on this step you leave all jealousies that have ever plagued you. All jealousies of any person or thing are now leaving you, and you already begin to feel lighter and better. You can now feel the loving warmth of that Upper Room, and its magnetic pull is becoming stronger each time a damaging emotion moves out of your life. You begin to realize that there is indeed Power in that room at the top of the stairs. The Great Consciousness is now pulling you to your assigned destination.

SIX All envy leaves you now. Put your mind to work on positive things. Start remembering when friends were happy and try to imagine yourself in their place, recreating that happiness within *you*. You cry of happiness and joy. You are no longer envious, for now you share their joys. You are becoming *one* with your Creation, and it begins to give you peace of mind.

SEVEN At this point separate yourself from your pride. No longer will pride dominate your life. Pride is a wretched thing. It hinders progress. It is a barrier to self-realization. It is a barrier to fulfillment. It is comparable to a wall between you and the knowledge you wish to acquire.

EIGHT You are now beginning to draw a curtain over your past, knowing that you can never change anything that has happened in your life. You have replaced all that is ugly and deceitful with love and understanding. You realize that the only changeable things are those which are in the present, so make the final gesture and close the curtain shut. Reject all that is in the past and start anew.

We are now halfway on the Seventeen Steps to our Upper Room. The first eight steps are what we call the Steps of the Negative Forces. You have now left these behind. They were difficult to climb, and you were forced to take a scrutinizing inventory of your inner self and recognize the reality within you. You are over them now, and the way is becoming easier. The following steps will be less steep and the progress faster. The magnetic attraction emanating from the Upper Room is getting stronger and stronger. Let's continue and climb.

NINE   Move forward and pause, to learn more about yourself. Self-realization is part of your mental-improvement course. Take a good look at yourself and single out something special that you feel needs improvement. Whatever it is, focus on it and imagine the need being the size of a marble. Now make it grow to the size of an orange, and you will see that it exceeds its self-imposed boundaries rapidly, expanding to the size of a basketball. Now it consumes you *completely!*

TEN   This step is very significant, for now you must think of all the good things in life that have come your way, not just yesterday, not just the day before, but during your entire lifetime. Go back, retrogress deep into your subconscious and try to recollect what brought you happiness, beginning from childhood until the present.

ELEVEN   Meditate on the good things you see happen to others and make them yours. List them, desire them, feel the need of them and claim them. Force them to happen to you, for they are yours to own.

TWELVE   Meditate on tomorrow and the days following. Imagine what would happen to you *if* everything you desire becomes reality. Flex your imagination and think, dream and accept, for imagination is a true basic form of psychic ability. Imagine how much richer, how much fuller and how much more important your life would be if you should LIVE love, not just *use* the word. Imagine having power; imagine possessing great wealth, more pleasant surroundings and true understanding with others. *Imagine* it, *desire* it, and it shall become yours.

THIRTEEN   Now, take the Love that you *know* fills the universe, mold it and let it absorb everyone who should partake of it. This time, do not give love to those who need it or to those who have hurt you. Let them become a *part* of the love that governs your actions. Let love take them and use them to make it grow. This step is one of the most positive of the seventeen.

FOURTEEN   You are now ready to climb the few remaining steps to position you into direct touch with the Creative Forces of the cosmos. Meditate for a moment, and see what has happened to you. You have accepted the existence of Someone higher than yourself. You have learned how to love yourself and how to love someone else. Because of this, you are now growing toward true perfection. You have come a long way; you are now ready to accept your true share of life. You are now ready to accept maturity.

FIFTEEN Concentrating on the realization of the respon- sibilities of maturity, you now take the fifteenth step and become mature. It has been building up within you; you have developed the ability to accept it. Realizing that it is yours and that it will influence all your actions from this day on, you are now being flooded with self-confidence. The reality of it overwhelms you. You are now grown up. You are now mature.

SIXTEEN Following the step to maturity, the one you are now climbing is responsibility. All lying, all cheating have gone. Integrity, honesty and sin- cerity have now filled your being, and you are closer to the Creator than you ever were before.

SEVENTEEN You have now reached the end of the stairway and are standing on the most important step. Following your upward-bound path of progress, you now expand your newly acquired maturity and responsibility and take the step to stability, experiencing the last phase of your preparation to enter the Upper Room. You have modified your basic emotions, climbing the seventeen steps. You will now undergo a thorough reshap- ing of your character. Only a short distance from you, well within reach, flow rivers of liv- ing water. You have found a new stability. Your fear is gone. Now, before you take the last few steps to the Upper Room, I want you to think of the many ways in which you can use your newfound stability. While you concentrate on what's ahead, standing on the threshold of the place of meditation, the magnetic pull emanat- ing from the Upper Room compels you to move forward, slowly—step by step. From the moment you cross the threshold you feel the Power. You feel charged with an energy that is completely strange to you. It's magnetic; all your senses respond to it. You feel drawn toward that comfortable-looking sofa sitting in the corner. You can't stop. You can't help yourself. All you can see is that sofa, and before long, you move over to it and lie down.

It is at this precise moment that you see the screen on the wall at the foot of the sofa. You know that you are not within the confines of a theater, but you wait nevertheless for those familiar flickering lights that usually precede a movie film. A soft glow begins to appear in the center and gently expands to the far corners of the pearly screen. You relax, but your mind is becoming inquisitive. The screen, your imagination, your eyes, they're all fusing into one, and you begin to see images.

What is it? What occupies your mind? Is it a flower? If so, can you smell it? Is it the fragrance of Creation that envelops you? Or is it a car? Do you actually feel the roar of the high-powered engine? Is it the odor of burning rubber as the car careens around the high-speed curves of the racetrack? Or is it a home? A friend? A loved one?

Really what *do* you see on the screen of your mind?

You slowly permit the images to penetrate, and then you relax. You are totally exhausted, and you need power more than ever before. With the screen now blanked out and your mind at rest, God takes over, and a sudden surge of power invades your body. God power is beginning to take possession of you, filling you with a degree of peace and confidence that you have never before experienced.

With peace and confidence comes perfection. Glancing back through your life, you may realize that it has been abused by you an incredible number of times. It is, however, still yours, filling your being with a tender glow. Now look at this perfection—just look at it—and imagine it as a slow, pulsating sphere of light. Strengthen it with your new-found power and watch it shine and grow, larger and larger. Watch it, for it is the waxing perfection within your being that is unfolding. It doesn't roll but just extends the span of its glow, cloaking you like a gentle, illuminating mist. Your entire self is now becoming one with the awesome presence of the God power. Perfection and you have now joined in a single holy union.

You are now at complete peace with the world. Purity has entered your life, and you are no longer the same person you were when you came into the room. All the cells in your body have become charged with God power, and subsequently, healing is taking place throughout your entire physical structure. Healthy cells now share their power with needy cells around them. Your body is changing, but so is your attitude. The power now moves through your mind. It affects your thinking. The *spiritual* You has triumphed over the unrestrained emotions of the *physical* You. It is this power that has effected the transformation. You know that as long as you live in harmony with it, it will always be your guide.

We have been to the mountaintop. We are now charged, and ready to face the world.

I'll walk with you while we leave the Upper Room and descend the Seventeen Steps. I'll walk with you while *you* meditate. Are you ready?

SEVENTEEN   I now accept a Superior Power. I am now wise because of it. I am now a pliable tool that can be used for the good of my fellow man.

SIXTEEN   I now accept the knowledge gained through my experiences leading to the Upper Room. Because of this, I know that I will gain more and greater insight.

FIFTEEN   I now accept this insight into matters affecting me and others. The curtains of my mind have been drawn back, and I am beginning to see with my spiritual eyes. The mist is lifting, and all is now clear.

FOURTEEN   I now have an abundance of health. The damaged cells within my body have been healed completely, and the cells of ill health no longer exist. My body will once again become sturdy and vibrant.

THIRTEEN   I now accept prosperity. Everything is here for me, and I must use my insight in deciding how to attain it and how to attract the material needs of my body. I am now able to attract and use those material gifts reserved for me.

TWELVE   I now have personality. Gone is my abrasiveness, my sarcasm, my shyness and anger. I will now display charm, warmth, goodness, consideration and love toward my fellow man. The new "me" is now being born and will be presented to the world as a new spiritual being.

ELEVEN   I am now humble, and because of this new magnetic character trait my kindness will be understood and accepted. My humility will identify me and will emphasize my self-confidence. I no longer have to resort to anger, for now I am one with God.

TEN   I am now strong. I have received strength because Eternal Power now vibrates through me. Every element of power within me now displays its full capacity, elevating my spiritual and mental character. My strength has helped me recognize my reason for being.

NINE   I am convinced that now I am here for a purpose. I want to fulfill that purpose, and I claim it as my own.

EIGHT   I now have a goal. I must busy myself about my Father's business. There are multitudes who need me, and I must let my purpose in life radiate from me so others can feel it and tune in to me.

SEVEN   I now possess great love. Knowing that love rules has filled me with love for God and for those around me. I *am* love. Love is now the dominant force controlling all my actions. It flows and glows and has made me lovely in the eyes of the Lord.

SIX   I am now energy. Every atom, proton and electron of my body is releasing its energy at my command, because my love wills it. My mind and body are in tune with my energy power, and my potential for good has multiplied a million times.

FIVE   I now have power. Ultimate power, because I am a child of the Almighty. Through love I now have the power to relieve suffering, cure heartaches, lighten burdens and release the power that will help others to become that which I want to become. I am like the flower whose buds are waiting for the refreshing rain so it can manifest itself in its fullest glory to the waiting world. With love's help, I can now unfold and show my power, for my power is love's power, and without it I cannot exist.

FOUR I now have understanding. Understanding is many things in one. It is power. It is quietness. It is serenity, but also kindness and mercy. It is one of the greatest manifestations of love.

THREE I now possess understanding of God and His creation. I not only understand my friends but my enemies as well, and will share with them my love and share with them their burdens that depress them. Their problems will become my problems, for I am now my enemy's brother.

TWO I now have ability, ability to recognize my talents and my gifts.

ONE I now recognize who I really am and what true psychic power means to me. I now know that since I have connected myself to this power, there is no turning back. I have tasted of its goodness, and I will grow and grow. I will become and become. I will never be the same again.

You now have at your disposal the time lock that will guarantee your entry into the infinite realm of the psychic dimension. Sure, I agree, the steps are mere words *but their effect is beyond description once the receptive mind is tuned in to them.*

If, after having given them the cynical scrutiny of your skeptical mind, you are still as determined as ever to become a novice, you might do well to check the following paragraphs and see what the steps have done for others who desired and *found.*

Mrs. D. R., New York, N.Y.

When, with two divorces behind me and one long painful stint in a mental hospital, I asked Mr. Bubar for help, he responded by sending me a tape with the "Seventeen Steps."

It has recreated me.

I was at the point of utter desperation when the steps entered my life, and twice a day I forced myself to concentrate on the seventeen steps. After each session another step became my own; *I claimed* victory over what it suggested. My confusion decreased, and I began to channel my emotions. What's more, however, I became susceptive to my husband's moods and desires. Incompatibility seemed to be the cause for all our disagreements before I started on the "Seventeen Steps." This now has made place for complete harmony because I am now able to anticipate his moods; I now feel intuitively what his emotional needs are. I now have begun to understand him and *feel* his probing love *actually* reach out for me. It's like both of us are now suddenly equipped with radar and "see" and "feel" without using our physical faculties.

Our children live once more in a house where harmony rules, and the threat of a divorce or another stay at the mental ward is completely out of the question.

Mr. K. B., Portland, Oregon

. . . I guess you could have called me a typical university student of the "new order" before I got hold of the "Seventeen Steps" recording. With my ragged-looking beard, uncombed shaggy hair down to my collarbones and with a marijuana weed between my lips whenever I could afford it, it was only a matter of time before I got hooked. It was the LSD that did it, for once I "reached beyond," I knew I needed it to live.

I heard about the "Seventeen Steps" and ordered them, curious at first, but fascinated once I tried them out. Ten days after meditating once a day I felt the urge for cleanliness and cut my hair and took a bath. Next on the list was the replacement of marijuana by love, real deep spiritual love for others, and it was not until I began to absorb the deep meaning of each one of the steps that my desire for the demonic visions caused by the use of LSD ceased. That was the moment when I sensed the true value of a period of true meditation with God.

Since I have made the steps my own I feel like a new man. I know now that I was in complete bondage to all my fears before. All my hangups are gone; my grades went from probation to a 2.7 average, and I have gained an insight in people that LSD could never have given me. I now proudly display the "peace" symbol, but for different reasons.

Mr. B. H., Chicago, Illinois

. . . the Upper Room is one place I couldn't do without. Since my acceptance of these steps I have set apart a special place in my plant (a small room, formerly a broom closet), for my meditations. My personnel know that whenever I go in there, I am not to be disturbed under any circumstances, for these two twenty-minute periods a day that I use for the "Seventeen Steps" are the most valuable ones in the entire twenty-four-hour period.

I know now there is power in sincere meditation, and twice a day I call a "board meeting" with myself after having climbed the seventeen steps and ask myself bluntly why I did certain things; why I made those unpopular decisions. I ask myself to give an account of every known business failure I have ever been involved in—and in the presence of God I open up and as a result new resolutions and impressions so real that it almost seems as if I can touch them come to my mind. When I leave the room I feel as if I can see "through" people. Their actions become an open book. As a result my losses have diminished; profit is up and my business has grown to what I call astronomical proportions.

Dr. F. G., Memphis, Tennessee

Speaking as a practicing psychiatrist, I must admit that you have worked a miracle with one of my patients. Your method has done things that normal psychiatry couldn't even think of accomplishing. Your steps have shortened her treatment and have given her insight and self-confidence. I am using your "Seventeen Steps" for several of my patients now.

And last but not least the words of a policeman who feels it has made his job one hundred percent easier.

With the increase in crime [J. L. of San Francisco writes], new methods will have to be found to not only *prevent* an even steeper increase, but to effectively *combat* the crimes that are already being committed. I found my newest weapon in the seventeen steps. It took me five full weeks, twice a day, to master the program, but once I had, and once I began to regard the Upper Room as my own, my activities began to change.

I am a new man when I walk my beat, for the uneasiness is gone; I now *know* where I am safe and where not. I have developed a sixth sense that tells me where to expect danger, and in what form. I am physically alert and it is beginning to show in my record of apprehensions. Knowing about people, "feeling" their intimate thoughts and "looking in" on their problems with the conviction that I actually *see* them psychically, has done much for me. For the first time in my life I am beginning to believe that it is possible to develop the whole man and not just the mere physical part.

There's no doubt that everyone's psychic. Your "Seventeen Steps" have cured my disbelief."

CHAPTER SIX

Psychic Principles and Business Affairs

Much has been said and written concerning the subject of positive thinking. Those who have practiced it will inform you that it works. Although it is not always the positive *thinking* that does it. It is the effect that positive thinking has on your emotional life that determines the success or failure of your attempts to put shape into your wavering affairs.

With the use of your psychic ability, no problem is too complicated to resolve. Through the years numerous businessmen have consulted me and confided their perplexities. "As a psychic, what do you feel I should do?" is their classic inquiry, and my reaction very often remains the same in most cases.

"Tune in to your problem," I advise them, "and you'll find the answer waiting for you."

"That's easy for you to say," you may remark, and I agree wholeheartedly; *however, if approached on the basis of the steps outlined under the Four-Step method, you can resolve your own dilemmas without the necessity of consulting a trained psychic.*

Some years ago, a businessman came to me vexed with the thought of losing his company. Wrong decisions, misjudged financial agreements, bankruptcy of certain customers—everything had converged on him at the same time, creating monetary and organizational havoc beyond description.

"What can I do, David?" he pleaded, while sitting disconsolately in my office. "I'm ruined!"

With our heads together, as if working on an intricate puzzle, we dissected his business piece by piece, examining each of his problems individually. But instead of providing him with a panacea, I gave him one simple bit of advice.

"Take your car and drive to Shiloh Park," I said gently placing my arm around his shoulder and guiding him to the door. "When you get there, find a quiet area and then just sit down. And no matter how long it may take, stay there and think of everything beautiful and serene that you can, but *forget* your problem. Only when you feel inner peace returning should you *then* examine your most urgent issue, and the answer will come to you."

He drove to Shiloh that day, and two hours later was ready to leave, a changed man. The tranquillity straightened him out, and his problems then seemed so insignificant and unimportant that his renewed self-confidence furnished him with just the mental edge he needed. Today he is one of the most successful businessmen I know.

In recollecting this experience, one thing stands out above all else. *He had tuned in to the God power, which gave him peace of mind,* and this in turn made him receptive to the answer he required. In our technological society, where everything proceeds according to which button is pressed or which dial has been turned, this can be bewildering, for tuning in to the God power is a mental process that results in spiritual connection and releases a type of energy of which our modern world has no concept.

The initial step to tuning in is the channeling of the mind's imagination into one single outlet, called *Concentration*. Visualize all the existing beauty. Imagine being a part of the harmony that inheres in the universe. Try to fathom the Love that created you and desire to be one with that Love. Think —think—think—until you experience a peace so totally overpowering, so vastly different from anything you have ever before encountered that you know you are now cupped in the hands of God and that whatever confusing problem faces you, it will be minute in comparison to the power of the One in Whose hands you are now held.

When this point is reached, you have cleared the first hurdle and have effectively brought into operation the beginning step of the four-step method, namely *desire*.

A peacefulness now enters your life, and you begin to seek after the answer to the perplexity that is plaguing you. Here a new element called *faith* is introduced to your world. Christ promised in Mark 11:24, "What things soever ye desire, when ye pray, believe that ye receive them, and ye shall have them." Can anything be more positive? Having *accepted* the Power of God, you now have a chance to *prove* His power simply by accepting His promise and believing that it will work.

Consequently, the second step of the four, called "Seek after it," is brought into operation, with faith in the outcome as the main drive. There is a condition, however, that you must fulfill before embarking on this problem-solving course. *You must have mastered your fear*. In a previous chapter, we touched on the elimination of fear, and only if this precondition has been met can you exercise faith. Faith has often been described as a sure belief in things unseen; fear, on the other hand, is the condition one experiences when unknown or ungovernable factors seem to threaten one's existence or way of life. Endeavoring to clear up a business problem—or any problem, for that matter—with fear as a constant companion will never work. Thus, by trusting fearlessly, by keeping all negative forces away and by believing that what you *need* will surely be granted, you have crossed the line separating steps three and four and are now prepared to accept the answer to your problem. Once accepted, the answer must be brought to bear on the problem at hand. In doing so, the four-step method not only will be concluded but also will have become a real part of you.

From my many discussions with harassed business executives, I have deduced that their overriding problem is usually not what they are complaining of but their inability to concentrate, to "tune in" to events surrounding the problem. Since these two factors are closely related, let me suggest a simple exercise that will flex your fledgling ability to "tune in" and "concentrate."

Select as a subject one of your close friends or a business associate. Sitting next to him, put all your energy to work, concentrating on him as strongly as you possibly can. "Tune in" to him and try to *feel* everything about him. Begin by thinking of the entire man; close your eyes and trace him in your mind. When you have succeeded in establishing his physical outline, try his mental image. What kind of a person is he? Is he kind? Considerate? Cooperative? Thoughtful? Have your mental beams probe his subconscious and fill you in on the *real* man. Don't give in and don't get discouraged; *continue* even if it takes ten, fifteen or thirty minutes. Suddenly you will reach the point where you will actually be on the same emotional plateau as he is. You will be able to start answering *your* questions concerning *him* from your own feelings, your own experiences. Without a warning, you will begin to feel his aches and his pains. His load will become yours. If his heart aches over insurmountable emotional problems, yours will ache with his. Through all this, you will be fully conscious and able to tune out at will. You have merely entered into a state of supersensitivity and are using this as a sophisticated probing device.

In the same way that each person is surrounded by a magnetic field that can be tapped and forced to release its information, situations too have their own invisible field surrounding them. Perhaps human emotions and decisions are the underlying cause for every happening; possibly when these emotions create problems, they have to be very intense, inevitably forming a separate force field. Detection then becomes unavoidable. The fierceness of these emotions also has another property—they further confuse the situation they have brought about in the first place. However, psychic force can be applied successfully to this situation, too. You can "feel" them out. It helps to have all the known facts at your disposal before beginning to evaluate your feelings, but to a trained psychic observer, this is not essential.

Psychic Principles and Children

I had the happiest home life a youngster could ever want. My earliest recollections date back to the years I spent in Blaine, Maine, a little nine-hundred-some-odd-people town, so restful and sleepy that even the chimney smoke wouldn't have risen if it hadn't had to.

I can well imagine the furor my birth must have caused on that wild snowy morning in March of 1928. The hands of the clock were stealthily moving toward 4 A.M. when Effie Turner, an aunt of mine who served as the community's midwife, was frantically passed the word to come and "get" me. It was indeed fortunate for me that they summoned her when they did, for when Effie finally arrived on the scene, I had just about strangled to death because of a twisted umbilical cord and had already turned a shade of bright royal blue.

But I survived, and that yellow two-story wooden house became my first home.

I was often told the story of how my mother bundled me up when I was only a few days old and proudly carried me into that little church to show me off to the anxious congregation and to permit my father to dedicate me to God.

It must have been an impressive service, for the old-timers still talk about it.

Drawing a comparison between King David and his own little son, my father solemnly began, "David slew Goliath, and slew the lions. The name of David means *beloved*. Today," he continued with a voice that rang out over the heads of the small but attentive congregation, "I am dedicating this child to God, and I am calling him David, for he will be a *modern* David. He will also meet his aggression and slay his lions, for he is truly chosen of God. God's hand is upon him and will always follow him, for he has been chosen to be a leader."

Psychic growth and leadership development is something that can be started at an early age, and he seemed to recognize this. When a child is still in his formative years, much attention should be given to increasing his general awareness and his sensitivity. A child has a running start on all of us when it comes to being close to the Source of Power. When working with children, this should never be forgotten.

The greatest educator of all times pointed this out when He said in Matthew 11:25, "I thank Thee, O Father, Lord of heaven and earth, because Thou has hid these things from the wise and prudent, and has revealed them unto babes." Because of their nearness to God and because they live under the cover of His revelation, infants begin life with far more sense than we often give them credit for. As they grow up, trust loses its position in the child's world, and uncertainty and fear move in.

We allow these things to happen, and many times even encourage it, yet the source of God power places intuitive knowledge far above the acquired wisdom we value so highly.

Children are basically psychic. Their ability to imagine is so real and so advanced that it can safely be regarded as a well-functioning sense. Their closeness to creation keeps their channels of communication wide open, and their intuitive power is so great that they can often see things with their spiritual eyes that may take adults years.

It was not until my sixth year that I began to realize that not everyone saw things the way I did, and it startled me. It was perfectly normal for me to hear music when there were no instruments or phonographs around. In those years, I did not consciously "tune in" to anything. Life tuned in to *me*, but I was not aware of it. Our house was always filled with the laughter and merrymaking of my brothers and me, but my closest companions were surprisingly not the members of my family but the voices of nature. I maintained contact with that part of God's creation on a twenty-four-hour basis. To me, butterflies were not just butterflies, they were little beings with whom I could communicate. I would talk to them as they fluttered from leaf to leaf, sharing my newfound knowledge with them. I would talk to the bees and worry for them if there didn't seem to be enough blossoms to go around. This communication was very one-sided, until one day I realized that they "spoke" to me, too, in their own special way. It made me the proudest boy alive to know that I had a secret friendship no one else could share.

For endless hours at a stretch, I would sit fascinated by the ants crawling around on the hill, and I would try to make myself known to them by attempting to think about their problems *their* way, living myself into their minuscule world. I admired them for their unwavering determination and wished I could be one of them until that dreadful day when I saw them deliberately crawl away from their nest on the hill to attack a dead mockingbird in an adjacent grass patch. I cried for hours that day, for I had never expected such ruthlessness on that beautiful hill.

The more I realized my aloneness, the wider the chasm between me and my boyhood chums became. I would see richly colored magnetic fields vibrating around people, and because of this, they appeared entirely different to me than they did to others.

Many times during those formative years I would separate myself from other children—even from my brothers and sister —and find a tranquil spot somewhere on the hill where our house stood just to sit down and think. And out of nowhere, again, would come that strange ethereal music, capturing me in its loving grip.

My psychic ability was always a part of me. Yet even before it manifested itself during those early years, my father knew deep down that I was different from his other sons, and it was he who brought the principles of faith, hope and charity into my life from the very start.

True psychic development in early life has to be built on these three principles. A child's faith far exceeds our wildest imaginings. This faith is the nerve that connects the creation to its Creator. Each child is a new creation and as such is pure and unblemished until touched by our tarnished hands. This must be avoided for our responsibility is not to *touch* but to *guide*. This guidance increases the child's faith and trust in God and man and expands its awareness of life, both here and beyond.

The second principle, hope, is one that is closely intertwined with a child's life. Never discourage a youngster from having hope. Never diminish the extent of his hope, for this is the first link between him and the future, and it can strengthen his entire relationship to the vast unknown world awaiting him. It also develops his intuition and imagination far beyond what he requires for survival.

But it is charity, love for his fellow human being, that will enable the child to convey his faith and hope to the world and establish for himself a secure haven in which he can safely live while using all his senses and all his capabilities. Teach these three elements to a child, and he will carry them into manhood and become more perceptive and sympathetic. When you encounter a person who has partaken of these principles during his early life, you will very likely find a psychic, for faith, hope and charity are the true attributes of a sensitive.

Mantle of Protection

When I think of the physical protection true psychic power can give a person, my mind inevitably retraces the events that caused June 12, 1967, to become the most calamitous day of my life.

That morning began as usual with Pat Dupree, my secretary, walking into my office and quietly taking her place behind her desk. To me, there was nothing out of the ordinary about this particular day, but to Pat, something seemed wrong. Periodically she would stop her typing, give me a long, examining look and then turn away and resume her work. Her interruptions became more and more frequent, increasing my uneasiness by the moment, until finally I swiveled around in my chair and stared at her. Then I realized why she had been watching my face; I was crying and hadn't even noticed. Wiping a tear from my eyes, I glanced at Pat, simultaneously glimpsing my tearstained face in the reflection of a framed photograph behind her.

"What's wrong, David?" she asked softly. "Why those tears?"

I wanted to answer her, confide in her, but I just couldn't. All I knew was that a heartrending sadness had taken possession of me. I sensed the foreboding of a tragedy so great, so intense, that it shook me to the core. Yet I didn't know why. I just stared at her and wiped my eyes again.

"I don't know, Pat," I said, my voice quavering with emotion. "I can't explain how I feel, but this I know. Someone very close to me is about to die. I have experienced these depressions before and remember them too well. But who is it this time? Who?"

Despondently I rested my head in my hands and started to think. Could it be someone close to me, or could it possibly be *me?* What was this fear that had so suddenly descended upon me—why today?

Impulsively I grabbed for the phone and called Beulah M. Vinsonhaler, the town manager of Blaine, Maine, the place where I was born and where my mother is buried.

I was through to Beulah within a few seconds, and being an old friend, I immediately divulged my premonition of death to her.

"You know, Beulah," I continued, "a person should always make funeral arrangements ahead of time, and I am wondering if you can check whether there is an empty space in our family plot. I've got to know."

"Now hold on to yourself, David," she soothed maternally, "nothing is going to happen to you, but I'll check anyway." A moment later she picked up the phone again. "Yes, there is space. Your father has provided for at least two other spaces besides the ones reserved for him and your mother."

"Reserve one for me, Beulah," I choked. "I'll probably need it shortly."

After a few restless hours had passed, I began to pack a light suitcase. I had to drive to Birmingham, Alabama, and then to Columbus, Georgia, where I was to visit with Charles

Smith, a psychiatrist friend of mine. I continued to feel that terrible anxiety, but now it was stronger, as if death itself was closing in fast.

I left my half-filled suitcase on the bed and called Colonel James Cooper, my attorney in Memphis.

"I've got the feeling that something may happen to me, Colonel," I explained hurriedly. "I have never written a will. Can you prepare one for me and have it ready so that I can drop by and sign it this morning on my way out of town?" He readily agreed, and I went back to my packing.

The heavy feeling still hovered over me while at the colonel's office, and after signing the will, instead of heading out of town, I found myself back at my front door. An hour later I started out *again* on my trip to Birmingham, turned the corner and drove two blocks. I made another turn and before I knew it, I had retraced my steps back into my driveway. The engine was still running when my secretary opened the door. Two more times I closed that front door and two more times I returned, the last time turning back at the city limits. On the fifth time around, I walked determinedly into my office, pulled a blank check from my pocket, signed it and handed it to Pat.

"Before I return, I see you taking a trip, Pat," I said. "I see you flying over trees and mountains. It is going to be a sad trip, and you'll need money. When you know how much, fill in the amount and give the check to Ed McCulley at the bank. He'll give you as much as you need."

With a final lingering look at the house, I drove off, stubbornly refusing to heed the dark premonitions that consumed me.

My business in Birmingham developed exactly as I had anticipated, and I departed late that evening for Columbus. It had been raining, and the black asphalt highway glistened as I zoomed on. The night was dark, and with the radio blaring to keep me alert, I had just reached the outskirts of Sel-lacuga, when suddenly, without warning, the back end of an old car appeared in front of me. Hitting it at a speed of slightly over seventy miles per hour, the impact propelled my car across the road and into a ditch. I knew I hadn't climbed out of the car, yet I found myself stumbling along outside with blood pouring down my face. Through a crimson haze I could see the faint glimmer of a dashboard light in the car and felt around in the front seat until I found my glasses. Strangely enough though, they wouldn't stay on my face. Then I knew I was hurt and hurt bad. I ran my hand up and down my face and around my head and experienced the weirdest sensation. My head was wet and quite symmetrical, without a nose or ears and completely hairless. Blood con-tinued to flow in torrents down my head and over my shoul-ders from what I later learned were two severed arteries. I noticed something resembling an oddly shaped hole in the windshield, and slowly the realization of what had hap-pened dawned on me. The impact had forced my head through the windshield, cutting off my nose and ears and en-tirely shearing off my scalp. Before the safety glass had a chance to spring back to normal, I had popped out and bounced back onto the front seat.

The warm blood soothed my shivers and I began to feel rested, almost comfortable. I leaned against the car and slowly sank to the ground. There was no pain now, only a re-laxed, contented feeling. I eased my head onto my hands and withdrew in horror, for there was nothing but bare bone and threads of flesh.

I heard a voice—it was my own.

"David," I asked myself, "what would you tell someone in the same circumstances?" and I knew the answer before I had even concluded my thought.

"Oh God, help me," I prayed. "You know my work isn't

finished yet. Send someone to help me. Send one of Your messengers to sustain me. Send physical messengers to aid me." I waited a few moments, and then added, "And I thank You now Father for what You are about to do."

I opened my eyes, and through the bloody mist I could see a car approaching in the distance. I yanked off my undershirt and staggered toward the middle of the road, waving my flag frantically, I thought, in the headlights of the oncoming car.

Hesitantly, the car jerked to a stop, and a horror-struck voice timidly called out, "Need any help?"

"Please get me to the hospital. I don't have much longer to live," and then my voice faded.

Mattie Powell and her son Roy, an Episcopalian priest, pulled me onto the back seat of their Volkswagen and raced toward the nearest hospital.

The car came to a screeching halt in front of the emergency entrance. A man, just leaving through the hospital doors, glanced at the car, hurried over to the window and peered inside. "This is what I have been waiting for," Dr. William Grammon declared. "Now I know why I felt that I shouldn't leave just yet!" and directing the nurses to transport me straight to the operating room, the world famous plastic surgeon took over. Under his austere supervision, a team of specialists labored until far into the night repairing the severed arteries, sewing my ears back in place, pulling the scalp to where it belonged and stitching my torn cheeks . . . in other words, just putting my head back into shape.

Lying in a semiconscious stupor following the operation, I began to realize the crime that I had committed—the act of ignoring the power of the mantle of protection. For many long years, I had been advocating and teaching people how to acquire this protective power, yet even though the warnings I received of my impending tragedy were numerous, I completely ignored them. My impressions, supported by the premonitions told me by some of my parishioners the previous evening, undoubtedly constituted a divine intervention.

Lou Harris, a woman who attended my church, had shaken my hand after leaving the service and implored, "I know you're going on a trip tomorrow—please don't! Something dreadful will happen to you if you go." Another woman, Corrine Williams, also warned me of the same imminent danger. "I'll be praying for you all the time you're gone," and still another parishioner, Beatrice David, also cautioned me, saying, "I see you in great peril tomorrow, Pastor Bubar. I wish you wouldn't go." And yet I went.

However, knowing that the accident would happen, God had already provided assistance. The Powells, my rescuers, had been visiting close friends that evening, and approximately a half hour prior to the time the accident occurred, Roy expressed his desire to leave. His mother was adamant and said no.

"It isn't time yet, Roy," she said, while listening seemingly to something unheard by everyone else except her. "The time isn't ripe yet."

Her clergyman son helplessly shrugged his shoulders, smiled and walked back to mingle again with a group of people. Within moments after her stubborn refusal to leave, his mother suddenly and persistently tugged at his arm.

"Something has gone wrong, Roy. I don't know what, but we must hurry out of here. Please son, hurry—hurry—" Quickly, they made their excuses, and throwing their coats over their shoulders, hastened to their waiting Volkswagen. It was here that both Mattie and Roy began to sense the dire urgency of their impetuous departure. Just beyond the city limits, the high beams of their headlights fastened themselves on a bloody, grotesque form staggering down the middle of the highway, grasping in desperation a blood-soaked rag he was feebly waving in front of him. Stopping their car, Mattie gasped to Roy, "Now I know why we were compelled to wait!"

Several weeks later I left the hospital—healed, but sure that this was the last time *ever* that I would consciously ignore a premonition and disregard the Power of Protection.

Premonitions of danger are nothing new, as we all know. Everyone has these intuitive fears about specific dangers that threaten a person's very existence. This is something that is inborn in every living being. I am convinced man was *not made* to die and the awesome power of death and the ominous aura of sadness that accompanies it can often be felt even before its presence is announced. Precognition, intuition, dreams, premonitions—they are the raw ingredients from which reality is made. Sparking creative thoughts, these impressions can become tangible if you set your conscious mind to work and react responsibly. Fear of death, the belief that one will die at a preassigned moment, and the waxing belief that the end is closing in are natural and not at all to be disregarded. It is one of nature's ways to inform us of the inevitable. It gives us a final chance to wrap up our lives. But—*and this may be the only possible way to lengthen our lives*—calling upon the power of the mantle of protection can often postpone the inevitable and loosen the tightening grip of death. Many of us know beforehand what will happen, but either refuse to listen to the voice of intuition or to make use of the mantle of protection. Yet we are guaranteed safety if we heed this voice and trust in a higher power.

"But whoso harkeneth unto me shall dwell safely, and shall be quiet from fear of evil," King Solomon once said, repeating a promise of God (Proverbs 1:33). This deals directly with the intuitive psychic power of man. It is the mind tuned in to the God power that gives us the deeper insight, the knowledge, the wisdom and the awareness. It is the God power

that gives us the mantle of protection and safeguards us *"from the fear of evil."* Nothing can harm us when we use this shield.

King David also knew of this protective force when he wrote Psalm 91, where it reads in verses 4 through 11:

"He shall cover thee with his feathers, and under his wings shall thou trust; his truth shall be thy shield and buckler;

"Thou shalt not be afraid for the terror by night; nor for the arrow that flieth by day;

"Nor for the pestilence that walketh in darkness; nor for the destruction that wasteth at noonday.

"A thousand shall fall at thy side, and ten thousand at thy right hand; but it shall not come nigh thee.

"Only with thine eyes shalt thou behold and see the reward of the wicked.

"Because thou hast made the Lord, which is my refuge, even the most High, thy habitation;

"There shall no evil befall thee, neither shall any plague come nigh thy dwelling.

"For he shall give his angels charge over thee, to keep thee in all thy ways."

Can anything be more realistic than God's mantle of protection, accompanied by angels with instructions to guard and attend? *This mantle of protection is all yours,* simply by tapping into the God power.

How can this be accomplished?

Strictly through the power of the mind, diligent training, and faith.

The only way an evil force can invade your psychic being is through thought power. No force can reach within you unless you grant it entry.

Through the will of the mind and the heart, you can draw a protective shield around you. In my own case, whenever I feel satanic influences closing in on me, I merely say, "I am now in God's Power. In the name of Jesus, protect me." I then retreat within myself and let the Power fight my battle. "Is that all there is to it?" you wonder. Yes. That's all, but to some people it is the most difficult thing to do, for it involves total submission to the superior power of a higher intellect. If I had invoked this power when the fearful anxiety of death focused on me, either I would not have started on my journey or the accident would not have taken place. Drawing upon God power and faith in the ability of that power to protect leads to a safer life, both spiritually and physically.

In our society, phenomena and reactions are not regarded as reliable unless they can be reproduced according to a specific scientific formula. Invoking the power of protection is no different.

When a witch like Sybil Leek wants to protect herself from the powers *opposing* witchcraft, she uses a sword and draws a circle on the ground and follows this by placing herself within this "sacred" area. This is supposed to safeguard her from the power of Good. Ironically she has borrowed this "circle" from those who in ancient times used it to protect themselves from the power of Evil. It was not the actual circle that did the trick; it was the mental approach that caused the person to draw the circle—a physical symbol of his acquired protective field—that saved him. For his need for protection and his plea to the forces of Good invoked that Power and protected him in time of danger.

This, then, is the principle upon which the power of the mantle of protection is built.

Before I give you some practical examples of how it worked for some of those who use it, let me outline several ways in which this power can be invoked:

(1) When you get an impression of impending danger for yourself or someone else, create a picture of that person in your mind, so clear that it seems as if you are actually

face to face with him. Next, imagine clouds of goodness, love and harmony around him. Imagine him being pure and just, still free of harm or danger. Then say loudly, "God power, protect [name] right now in this hour of great need through Divine intervention," and then imagine an invisible cloak of protection being dropped over him. Imagine this cloak to be the actual mantle of protection that God is draping over him. Then just *accept* the fact that he *is* being protected from that moment on. Your doubting the effectiveness of your action will destroy what you have just done.

(2) When you receive definite impressions of danger or illness regarding yourself, draw a mental picture of yourself and then imagine an actual sphere being drawn around you. Next imagine this giant bubble being filled with nothing but love, pure love, and think of it drifting on the rippling water of a quiet secure harbor. Then, and only *then*, say: "I now invoke the protection of God around me. No danger will befall me."

(3) Being a minister, I have found great strength in using the 91st Psalm as a source of protection. I know many people who, when in danger or when going out on a dangerous military mission, meditate for twenty minutes on the Seventeen Steps and follow this by placing their faith in all the promises God has laid down in the 91st Psalm. It worked for David, it worked for Solomon, and it will work for *you*, for God's promises are for everyone.

Gratifying are the many testimonies that reach my office as a result of dedicated psychic novices following the recommended steps for development and extensive use of the mantle of protection.

Not so long ago I received a letter from a woman in Missouri who had awakened with the strange feeling that this could very well be her last day. "I didn't know exactly when and how," she explained, "but I knew something was about to happen." She was an organist and had an appointment to play for a wedding that afternoon. All through the day, the uneasy feeling of death became more intense. When she entered her car to drive to the wedding she couldn't bear it any longer.

"I then invoked the mantle of protection around me," she continued in her letter, "and even though still depressed, I drove off. Nothing happened until I suddenly felt impelled to stop at a service station at the edge of town." While tanking up, she asked the attendant to check her wheels. A few minutes later, a slightly puzzled mechanic peeked into the window.

"Ma'am," he said, "all your wheels are okay except the front right one. It's loose. I don't know who's got it in for you but four of the five bolts that hold the wheel in place are missing, and the last remaining bolt has already worked itself halfway out."

"I may not be a well-developed psychic," she wrote in closing her letter to me, "but I have surely decided never to travel without first assuring myself of the presence of the mantle of protection. It saved my life."

The mantle of protection works not only in cases of pending physical harm but also in business dealings of an honest man. A friend of mine in Illinois had spent many years building a highly profitable business, but with retirement around the corner, he was eager to sell. The offer was $1,500,000. He was *ready* to sell, but first invoked the power of the mantle of protection around him to be sure he would not lose unjustly what he had gained with honest business methods.

Several days later, half an hour before the closing of the deal, the buyer's attorney suddenly became ill and forced a postponement. The next appointment, too, fell through, because of internal friction within the buyer's company. Within a day after that, the entire deal was called off.

You wonder what the mantle of protection did here? It became apparent ten days after the initial closing date. *The seller had been willing to take the purchase price completely in the stock of the new owner's parent company; but that stock hit rock bottom, and the stock he would have acquired as a result of the sale of his business would have dropped from $1,500,000 to less than $200,000.*

Today the man still has his business, and his earnings have climbed to $250,000 per year. Surely the mantle of protection was at work here!

Many illnesses are psychosomatic, or caused by other than external physical influences. Such was the case with Michael Festes, sales manager of the American Bottling Company in New York.

Molly Festes, his wife, called to tell me that Mike had been taken to the hospital complaining about severe headaches, which at times left him partially paralyzed. Every test negative, his attending physicians were ready to give up and wait for the inevitable. Molly called me and begged for help.

"Molly, let's pull a mantle of protection around him," I suggested, "for if the cause of his illness can't be found then there must be other elements at work.

"I want you to go to the hospital and stand by his bedside. Don't say a word to him, but slowly move your raised hands over him from his head down to his feet, and while doing this, say 'Thank you, Father, for what you are about to do. Thank you, Father, for Your mantle of protection.' *Don't ask for healing;* ask for God's *protection.* Once protected by *faith* in His power, nothing can harm him.

"Next, I want you to read the Psalm of Protection, the 91st Psalm, and end it by saying 'Thank you, Father, for your protection.'"

Molly Festes did just that, and within days, Mike was out of the hospital, headaches gone and armed with a renewed faith in the God power.

Psychic principles do work. They're not just hollow phrases with which to pacify the weak of mind. Those who believe and have tested them know the power they can reveal. The power of the mantle of protection is only one of the many manifestations.

CHAPTER SEVEN

Among the hundreds of letters that pour into my office each day are many that express a thorough concern for humanity in general. Many express utter desperation; others are filled with problems of a more personal nature. Some questions that keep repeating themselves in the course of a year are such that I should like to share them with you. They correctly reveal the problems of the times and the doubts and perplexities that plague people today.

The quest for understanding has reached unusual heights in recent years. Some of our most popular television programs deal with expressions of human misery and the ways in which these miseries are being handled. Yet the suffering still increases. Most of our popular songs, whether they be country, western or more sophisticated, are based on the theme of loneliness. "Love me—understand me—don't leave me—" they cry, and around these words modern lyrics are built. The more agony a song writer can put into his words, the better the chances are of reaching millions. Loneliness, fright, uncertainty, infidelity, these are concepts on which business empires are being built, simply because every one of us is subject to at least one of these feelings and wants a way out.

Everyone, whether he writes me or prefers to keep his anxieties locked up within himself, is harassed. Humanity cries out for understanding, and whereas God, to many people, seems to be a rather distant figure, they do not hesitate to share their burden with a perfect stranger, hoping to find the way to peace of mind.

Mrs. H. G. of New York writes:

"Do you believe in reincarnation—and if so, to what extent?"

There is much being said, taught and practiced today in regard to reincarnation. As a matter of fact, many of our leading mental institutions are filled with people who firmly believe that they are incarnations of Cleopatra, Mozart or even Jesus Christ. Not a single day passes that a new Napoleon or Einstein doesn't join the ranks of the mentally disturbed, but unless they are officially committed to these institutions, they are regarded as "incarnations" of those who lived before—at least in the eyes of the "believers." That a mere piece of paper with the signatures of the guardians, relatives or a judge signifies the thinly defined boundary between insanity and reincarnation is enough cause for alarm.

A business executive told me recently that he had at last discovered who he had been in his former life.

"John the Baptist, that's who," he exclaimed proudly, and when I asked him why John, he replied that he was tormented with fainting and choking spells and that John must have felt the same way when he was beheaded. I could have told him of the young minister who came to me for counseling and ultimately confided that it was only natural for him to be a minister, as he was in reality an incarnation of John the Baptist. "I am not just a minister," he admitted, "but I am the forerunner of a new great Christian leader." And I could have told him about that letter I had received from Cincinnati, Ohio, written by a woman who claimed she had only been a woman since she was born "this" time. "I was John the Baptist before," she wrote proudly! And for a moment I even thought of telling him about my telephone conversation earlier that day with a schoolteacher from Wisconsin who had called to tell me who he had been in a former life. Yes, you've guessed it—John the Baptist!

I am vigorously opposed to the idea of reincarnation for many reasons. I do not deny that the cycle of life is real and that a certain degree of evolvement is necessary and that natural laws do exist, but some confuse reincarnation with the life cycle of a tree—and that's where all comparison fails.

"A seed is planted," they say, "and grows into a tree. After leafing, seeds of the tree drop to the ground, then germinate and grow and develop into another tree." Yet to me, this does not at all signify that the tree has "become" all over again. The first tree will never exist again, but the results of its life will always live on.

In Hebrews 9:27, the apostle Paul states pointedly that, "It is appointed unto men once to die, but after this, the judgment."

There is a limit to life, and only after the final judgment does man live eternally. Because of their constant search for excuses and reasons to justify their erratic behavior, many people feel compelled to believe in reincarnation. It offers the Great Escape for those harassed with emotional weaknesses, guilt and laziness and those who suffer from a lack of correct information. To them reincarnation is the mill that grinds out principles they need in order to believe that a "past life" can help solve all the mysteries of the past present and future.

There is a type of reincarnation that is real but only if it is brought down to the level of energy. Energy will always exist, yet it is more a matter of continuous existence than it is of renewed existence. On many occasions I have counseled with individuals who are positively convinced that their evil acts were predestined to be committed by them because of their "behavior" in a previous life. Many others come to me seeking my help to identify their former incarnation.

Regressing into the human past solves no problems and produces no spiritual heights. One never goes backward in order to arrive at a forward position. I am also asked, "Isn't it necessary to come back again in another body so that we can learn what we neglected in our previous life?" Of course it isn't. Just because you didn't digest everything you were supposed to in the fourth grade is no reason for you to return to that grade all over again. There are a multitude of things we never learn.

Sure, don't get me wrong; I too want to survive, just like you. But to believe that my future would consist of nothing but a continual reincarnation into an endless row of physical bodies would in itself bring nothing but utter despair, unsurpassed hopelessness and everlasting hell. A great many of those who have persuaded themselves that they have been reincarnated are merely granting unclean spirits to possess, influence and obsess them.

Miss R. B. of Los Angeles, asks:

"Do you ever get any insight into the future through dreams?"

I most certainly do. I can't recall the number of times when a dream I had turned out to be an almost exact replica of what eventually did happen. But then, this is nothing new. Joseph was a dreamer, and so was King David and many other figures of old.

Cruden's *Complete Concordance* states: "The belief in dreams was generally connected with consultation of idol priests, or those pretending to deal in magic. The Israelites were warned against dealing with them. But God revealed His will frequently in dreams, and there were those who could explain them."

Many dreams are symbolic, and need careful interpretation before they can be of any use. If you start out from the basic premise that a dream is your subconscious talking to you, telling you certain facts in symbolic language, then you are making a step toward interpretation. Sometimes, however, these "symbolic messages" are so strong and so vivid that the dreamer practically knows the meaning of the dream immediately. Some of my dreams are almost as vivid as my conscious experiences. Take the one I had about hurricane Camille, the prediction that also came to me in a flash vision. In my dream I saw a disastrous and destructive storm strike the Gulf Coast, demolishing Biloxi, Mississippi, and killing hundreds of people. When the hurricane finally hit, I checked and became aware that the same buildings I had seen destroyed in my dream had actually been flattened by the storm!

The outcome of the 1970 Alabama election electing George Wallace for governor was revealed to me in a dream, too, even before he had publicly announced his candidacy. Another interesting dream was the one I had about a friend of mine, a politician in a city on the East Coast. I woke up extremely disturbed and called him the same day.

"Ray, are you by any chance planning on getting married?" I asked, point-blank. "I have dreamed something very disturbing about you and want to make sure I am not imagining things."

He sounded surprised and admitted that he was planning to marry a girl he had known for only a few months. I asked him for a description, and as he described her, I could see her all over again, the same way I saw her in my dream, holding a gun, using dope and working as a professional prostitute.

"Check on her carefully, Ray," I advised him. "Don't ask me why. Just do it."

Twenty-four hours later he called back, excited and upset.

"Just got the report in," he stammered. "She's been married four times and every one of her husbands died under mysterious circumstances. On top of it she's been working as a prostitute in many states, has several convictions for peddling narcotics and is out on bail right now pending a hearing in a southern state. David, marrying her would have ruined my career!"

A dream? Yes, but one for the books!

I am quite adept at interpreting my own dreams, but when it comes to explaining someone else's, I feel inept, as I am not able to judge other people's inner struggles and emotional crises. There are some good books available that might help you find the answers to some of your most perplexing symbolic dreams.

Don't discard your dreams as fantasy. Remember, they are caused by your subconscious mind. Perhaps you are trying to tell *yourself* something.

The recent psychic rage undoubtedly influenced J. L. of Detroit, Michigan, for he queried:

"Do you ever use any devices such as shiny surfaces or automatic writing?

No, I do not; however, this does not indicate that others may not feel the necessity to utilize them. I have observed someone holding a pencil in his hand, and while his mind was completely detached, his hand wrote faster than the human eye could follow—certainly faster than normally possible, because an outside entity (evil spirit) had seized control of him. This is called *automatic writing*, because the invisible controlling force dominates all conscious and subconscious actions of the subject.

Impressional writing is another form of automatic writing where the writer is aware of what he is writing, yet is completely powerless to exert any influence over it. *Inspirational writing* is when an individual receives direct *thought inspiration* and writes accordingly. The Bible aptly states in 2 Timothy 3:16, *"all scripture is given by inspiration."*

Space travel has stirred the imagination of many and aroused the interest of J. P. in New Orleans, who asked:

"Mr. Bubar, will we ever be able to travel astrally? Have you ever traveled this way?"

It is sometimes extremely difficult to distinguish between astral projection, dreams, visions or a genuine clairvoyant experience. I recall how one morning at 2 A.M. I awakened rather suddenly, and impulsively grabbed a pencil and paper from the nightstand beside my bed. I had just "dreamed" something, and it had seemed so realistic that I was willing to believe I had actually been there. In my dream, I had been wandering about in a combat area somewhere in Germany when a battle-fatigued GI drew near and gave me his name.

I hurriedly wrote it down and went peacefully back to sleep. The following morning I located a friend in the local phone directory and asked him if he had ever known a GI answering to the description of the man I had seen in my dream. He had indeed. It was a close friend of his, who had been killed during one of the major battles of the Second World War.

Was it astral projection? I prefer to regard it as a contact with energy forces that are still intact.

As I was meditating in my Upper Room a few months ago, a situation occurred that I *feel* was astral projection. I was in a relaxed frame of mind and felt completely detached from my surroundings. Glancing about me, I noticed a boy in army uniform and walked up to him. After conversing for a moment, I began to observe the immediate vicinity, which appeared to be Vietnam, together with visible landmarks and other identifying marks. *Two weeks later I encountered the same boy physically, but this time it was in the U.S.A.* After comparing notes, he was absolutely convinced that I had indeed been there, for the landmarks I described could only have resulted from personal observation!

Astral projection was a frequent happening during the time of the biblical prophets. Ezekiel experienced it quite regularly. An example of this is found in Ezekiel 11:1. *"Moreover, the spirit lifted me up and brought me unto the east gate of the Lord's house."* St. John also communicated with God in His domain, as did many other prophets.

From Memphis, Tennessee, came a letter from Mrs. L. F. containing the following inquiry.

"Do you equate yourself with Peter Hurkos?"

Although I am familiar with the name and reputation of Peter Hurkos, I am not able to compare my ability with that of his. Our fields of endeavor are miles apart. He is primarily interested in criminal investigations and the nightclub circuit, and I am more occupied with personal spiritual counseling and am basically interested in developing and using my God-given talents for the aid of mankind. Most of my talents are related to treating the results of mental and spiritual neglect. It is my contention that if the mind and spirit of man can be healed, the physical body will attune itself to the impulses of the vital life forces within. I claim no ability of myself. I would rather be viewed as an instrument through which God power can flow. Everyone should find his own gift and talent and learn how to use it rather than pattern himself after someone else.

From Memphis also, a Miss W. S. asks:

"What are your beliefs in the use of the zodiac signs?"

Astrology is one of the oldest practices of the occult. I do not wish to be classified as an expert on astrology, for I place more value on direct contact with the Higher Power of the Universe than on numbers, birthdays, planetary actions or signs of the zodiac. It is reasonable to assume that certain planets do exert a degree of attraction on the earth as does the moon; however, even if some people erroneously believe that this is the way to contact God, why go that route when direct communication with Him through prayer is available? I have witnessed too many lives where growth has been deformed because of misplaced faith in astrological forecast instead of belief in the great power found in the Bible. Many strange things do happen during the full moon that do not occur at any other time, but these areas are still open for scientific investigation.

Mr. B. C. of Portland, Oregon, writes,

"Does God really exist, and if so, how do you intend to prove it?"

If you do not believe in God, you most certainly cannot believe in the Bible, so let us approach the subject from pure logic. There are many reasons why one should believe in an all-caring, all-loving God. If the Christian claim is true that no one can escape His control even for a fraction of a second, then it is essential for us to know more about this Power.

We know that we exist, but we also know that we had nothing to do with our own entry into existence. We must therefore have been caused by a power than can cause bodies to appear, intelligence to become apparent and discernment to become obvious. We are personal beings, not an impersonal mass of intelligence. Is it then reasonable to assume that an *impersonal* force created that which is *personal;* that an unintelligent source produced that which can think and respond? The world is filled with people like ourselves, and whenever there is too much of one thing to be a freak of nature, there must have been a common cause behind their being. Floyd E. Hamilton in *The Basis of Christian Faith* (Harpers) said, "The processes of birth are not sufficient to account for us. Physiology tells us that the body of the mother, while it supplies blood to the embryo, apparently has no active part in the formation and growth of the tiny body in the womb, much less of the soul itself. All the human body does is to *transmit life which it did not produce!*"

In *The Philosophy of Theism* (Harpers), Borden P. Browne states, "As there is no way of deducing intelligence from non-intelligence, so there is no known way of deducing the moral from the non-moral." A moral man must have a moral cause as his maker.

Two other sections in *The Basis of Christian Faith* demand to be heard. On page 48 Floyd E. Hamilton writes, "Plan and purpose are characteristics of our own mind and when we find them about us in 'nature,' do they not indicate that the

Cause of the universe is capable of purposive thinking? The fact that different kinds of liquids crystallize into different but regular shapes of crystals, indicates plan and purpose. The fact that when water freezes it begins to expand just before the freezing point, shows design, for were it not so, the lakes would freeze to the bottom and a real glacial period would envelop the world. The fact that cells in plants and animals divide according to plan points to a rational Cause. If the temperature of the earth's surface were to rise only a relatively few degrees, life would be impossible. Does not this indicate design by a Cause who thinks?"

On page 49, he continues his argument. "A beautiful sunset is not a chance happening. The separation of the different colors of the rainbow through refracted light; the harmony of natural colors; the music of birds and the waterfall; the majesty of a storm at sea; the bursting of the petals of the rose; the delicate scent of the violet; all point to a Cause who planned such things for the enjoyment of mankind as a manifestation of His own glory. The laws of music and the diatonic scale point to a Cause who creates music. Only a planning Person could produce all these things."

Does God exist? He most certainly does, and in the face of the available irrefutable evidence, all I can do is be thankful and worship and admire the Cause that made all things possible.

The question of auras has always fascinated people. Mrs. P. L. of Dayton, Ohio, is no exception. She asks:

"Do you ever see auras? Do animals see auras?"

Many people devote endless hours in an attempt to envision an aura around someone's head. The existence of halos is to me completely certain. Ofttimes, in old paintings, the artists's conception of early saints was depicted with a luminous glow about their heads, a glow which we call a halo. It may be possible that their highly advanced degree of spirituality caused a glow to form around them. Many artists, sensitive as they are, may actually have seen this glow and captured it on the canvas. Because of a serious lack of deep spirituality, most of us do not see these radiant halos. Everyone has his own aura, but I do not look forward to the day when, through new scientific methods, these magnetic rays can be made visible at will. Each character trait casts a different glow, and their visibility will betray everyone's true personality and intentions.

Seeing auras is not limited just to us humans. Mice, dogs and many other animals have that ability, and I firmly believe that the higher spiritual person is able to "feel" the character and disposition of a person rather than having to look for their aura.

A letter from G. F. of Medford, Massachusetts, revealed this question:

"What is the cause of the experience where you know you have done something before or have been somewhere previously, but you actually haven't?"

Many people uphold the conviction that they have lived in another life and were reincarnated. I often "hear" music, and being a semiprofessional piano player, I sit down and play what I've heard, but I definitely do not feel that I must be either Beethoven or Bach reincarnated because I play their music. Yet how am I able to play some of their compositions before I have even listened to them with my physical ear?

The answer to me is quite evident. Energy cannot be destroyed, and sound is energy. We must realize that encompassing everyone is this "memory" of sound and energy in motion. Some are gifted and talented enough to be able to tune in to such channels as are needed for medical knowledge; others are more interested in the musical knowledge stored up in the memory bank of time.

The tuning in to historical events, places and times is a coming thing in this generation; but this does not mean that one actually is uncovering proof to substantiate the pagan doctrine of reincarnation.

A once-in-a-lifetime question by Miss S. H. of Washington, D.C. reached me several weeks ago.

"Are ghosts sexless and do they have the ability to procreate?"

Not having been "there," I know less than hearsay about this subject. We must realize, though, that sex in reality is only a thought. One cannot engage in a sexual relationship without thinking about it first. Therefore, if sex is a thought and thoughts are also a part of what we know as the "spirit world," then some may argue the point that there is a place for sex in that realm. However, Matthew 22:30 states in connection with this, *"For in the resurrection they neither marry, nor are given in marriage, but are as the angels of God,"* indicating that if there is sex, it will no longer occupy a predominant place. If there is to be procreation after the resurrection then this may be accomplished asexually.

"Do ghosts procreate?" you ask. Honestly, I doubt it. And this I am sure is as far as anyone would dare to venture.

Mrs. M. D. of West Hollywood, Florida, asked:

"What does imagination have to do with psychic ability?"

No greater asset is possessed by man than the power of his imagination, yet it is the least understood of all human faculties. A mental image is always the blueprint for everything that is being made. Imagination is the power that forms an idea and then projects it into the world. It is a creative and a spiritual power. Through imagination we can change hate to love; despair to success; disease to health. Imagination can also be called a transformer of the soul.

Jesus made use of instantaneous manifestation through imagination. He turned water into wine and caused many other miracles to happen through first imagining in the mind what was needed and how the need could be alleviated. In fact, it is in the Bible, in Genesis 1:26 where imagination was first put to the test. "... *let Us make man in Our image, after Our likeness*," God said, and His Word brought His imagination to life.

A letter from a Mr. L. P. of Birmingham, Michigan, brought one of the most popular questions that people ask today.

"What do crystal balls have to do with foreseeing the future?"

The crystal ball is used merely as a point of concentration, being an ideal crutch for those without adequate powers of the mind. The ancient prophets used shiny stones that were sewn onto their clothing or hung around their necks as points of concentration. It is at the moment of total concentration that one becomes subject solely to God's influence.

I do not use a crystal ball. However, there are many who do and who regard it as one of the most effective instruments of the psychic world. In reality, it is only a crutch, a means to an end. It adds to the mystery and introduces an object that can be used as a topic of conversation as well as an object of concentration, but it most certainly does not supply a God-approved instrument as mediary between God and man. The use of a crystal ball is more psychological than anything else.

The practice of crystal gazing was common in ancient Egypt, and it is interesting to note that it was there that paganism flourished more than in any other world empire.

In recent years, the connection between idol worship, devil worship, satanic practices and the crystal ball has become more subtle, and once again, the crystal ball has received the reputation of reliability without any justification.

Crystal gazers have their own language and terminology to describe what they claim is revealed to them in the magic sphere. A vision of a coffin, for example, is curiously interpreted by them as denoting a speedy marriage; a cow indicates prosperity; a cradle has a definite connection with family increase; dice mean scandal and dishonor, and so on.

There have been many efforts through the years to link the breastplate of the Jewish High Priest of biblical times to the crystal ball, but corroborating evidence for this theory is nowhere to be found. The priest wore the Urim and the Thummim, two special stones, whenever he went into the temple to beseech God for an answer to problems facing Israel. Through these stones God would signify His will. Again, however, *there is no Biblical indication that these stones were the Jewish equivalent of the pagan crystal ball.*

"Is there intelligent life outside our solar system?"

This question was mailed in by Miss L. L. of Topeka, Kansas, and deserves a good answer.

The Bible gives us no conclusive answer to this question; thus we must turn to scientific investigation.

Modern science enabled us to penetrate the black unknown of the universe with radio telescopes, so sensitive and so precise that they can pick up cosmic signals from one hundred light-years in space.

Dr. Harlow Shapley, Harvard professor emeritus of astronomy, has worked out some interesting statistics on the probability of intelligent life in space.

According to his calculations, the number of stars we can "listen" to with our modern radio telescopes can be estimated at the *number 10, followed by nineteen zeros.* "Of this unthinkable number," he was asked, "how many stars have planets rushing about them?" His answer: "One in a thousand." Of these "one-in-a-thousand" worlds, again one in a thousand will lie just the right distance from its sun so that a moderate temperature can sustain life. Of these planets, Dr. Shapley says, one in a thousand will be large enough to bind and keep an atmosphere. He applies his one-in-a-thousand ratio once more when asked how many of this vastly reduced number will have the proper atmosphere with the right amounts of hydrogen, nitrogen, carbon and oxygen to support cellular life such as exists on earth. Cutting the total number of stars that can be "seen" with the radio telescope this way still leaves us with *one hundred million planets in the universe on which some kind of life is not only possible but probable.*

In 1959, a determined effort was made to try to establish contact with some of these "possible" planets through a new radio telescope constructed at Green Bank, West Virginia. The communications attempt, known as Project Ozma, was aimed at contacting the star Tau Ceti. The distances involved, however, are so enormous that the signal beamed at Tau Ceti in 1959 took eleven years, traveling at a speed of 186,000 miles per second. This means that now, in 1970, Tau Ceti may be able to listen in on the first communication from earth. But, if the inhabitants should decide in turn to contact us the same day they receive our signal, it would again take eleven years at 186,000 miles per second to get their message across. And this is only *one* of the 100,000,000 stars in our galaxy that are capable of supporting life as we know it.

The probability of other life in our galaxy is supported by Mrs. E. G. White, whose inspired pen wrote an account of one of her early visions.

"The Lord has given me a view of other worlds," she writes in *Early Writings* (Review and Herald Publishing Association). "Wings were given me and an angel attended me from the city to a place that was bright and glorious. The grass of the place was living green, and the birds there warbled a sweet song. The inhabitants of the place were of all sizes; they were noble, majestic, and lovely. They bore the express image of Jesus and their countenances beamed with holy joy, expressive of the freedom and happiness of the place. I asked one of them why they were so much more lovely than those on the earth. The reply was, 'We have lived in strict obedience to the commandments of God, and have not fallen by disobedience, like those on the earth.' Then I was taken to a world which had seven moons. . . . There I saw good old Enoch, who had been translated."

Would it not be supremely egotistical to believe that we are the sole intelligent beings in the entire universe?

Considering how many psychic "toys" are being sold in the stores nowadays, the following question had to arise. It did. Miss T. F. of Oklahoma City, Oklahoma, writes:

"What do you feel about the Ouija board?"

Not so long ago, after concluding a talk on psychic affairs to a group of high school students, one of the listeners told me about her experiences with the Ouija board. Her story is certainly worth repeating.

"A few weeks ago, on a Saturday night to be exact, my girl-friend and I were experimenting with the Ouija board," she explained, "and the clarity with which the answers to our questions came made us wonder as to the identification of the intelligences operating it.

"We held onto the board and asked, 'You who answer—who are you *really*?'

"The answer was tapped out with amazing speed.

"'The Devil.'

"We were terribly shaken but continued.

"'Can we meet you?' It may have been a stupid question—for whoever wants to meet the Devil?—but we treated it like a game and played along.

"'Yes!' came the reply.

"'Where?' we queried.

"'You name it. . . .' the Intelligence responded. We named a street corner not too far from our home and informed the board.

"When we asked what time, the words came back 'Three A.M.,' and then the contact was broken.

"And at 3 A.M. the next morning, my girlfriend and I sneaked out of the house and drove to the appointed corner. There in the darkness stood a solitary figure, wearing a long coat with the collar turned up, impatiently glancing from side to side.

"Was he our man? I am sure we will never know, for we didn't stop to ask!"

This experience, I am certain, is one of many, for more than four million Ouija boards have been sold in the last two years alone. Ouija, a combination of the French and German words for *yes* was invented in 1890 and has had a gigantic surge of popularity since the end of World War II.

In April, 1970, *Cosmopolitan* magazine published a lengthy article entitled "The Ouija Board Speaks—Are You Listening?" and in the words of parapsychology writer, Hans Holzer:

"This Ouija thing is a workable gateway to the unconscious. It may very well be harmful if the person using it is unaware he or she is possessed of deep trance psychic abilities.

"What sometimes happens if a person is receptive to a spirit is that spirit will enter his body through the medium of the Ouija board and perhaps possess him so completely that the receiver's will is totally blotted out. . . . A child, a virgin, a sexual innocent is especially susceptible to being possessed. I know of a number of people who have been entered through the Ouija board, and let me tell you it's a difficult and tedious task to rid an involuntary medium of a spirit. The outcome will often be schizophrenia or some other form of mental illness." Most theologians and psychiatrists tend to agree with him.

The struggle for physical survival is basic to every human being, and it is tragic that in our beautiful world, Mrs. G. A. of Plymouth, Massachusetts feels forced to ask:

"Do you think there will be peace in our lifetime? Not only in Vietnam but in all the world?"

Ultimate peace will be just an illusion for many years to come. Tranquillity and harmony between nations is the result of peace of mind.

The events now transpiring in the world have been prophesied a multitude of times in various books of the Bible. Matthew 24 is especially specific in relation to this.

The disciples asked Christ about signs of the end of the world and of His second coming. His answer as recorded in the entire chapter of Matthew 24 and in other references reveals that peace will not be ours to claim until after the expiration of the following calamities.

• *Tremendous earthquakes as never before in history:* In connection with this, it is proper to note that since 1950 more than 180,000 people have lost their lives as the result of earth upheavals in various parts of the globe. Never before has there been such a rapid sequence of quakes.

•*Famine and pestilence:* The number of victims here will never be known. In 1919, the great famine in China claimed, according to some reports, several million people. In three provinces alone, there were more than thirteen million people homeless and starving.

Referring to the great Russian famine that closely followed the Chinese tragedy, the Archbishop of Canterbury declared that "never in the history of the world has a condition of things existed comparable to the ghastly death by famine of whole millions of men, women and children."

Present starvation conditions in India, Africa and other world areas are swiftly approaching the total reached in those two deadly famines. Even today, experts testify that within a short number of years, the world population will far exceed the availability of food, causing wholesale starvation again.

Pestilence, although partially under control, is still raging throughout many sections of the world. In 1918, when the common influenza held the masses in its grips, no one at first took it seriously, but, before its initial rampage had been brought under control, millions had died. Conservative estimates based on reliable reports place the number of flu deaths in the world during that epidemic at roughly between fifteen and twenty million.

Today, most of the once-dreaded diseases are under control, but subconsciously we seem to be overanxious to help fulfill this prophecy. Diseases have been invented and "condensed" in our war laboratories, so terrible and so unspeakable that we may well be in a position to completely fulfill the biblical prophecy during the next world war.

•*Increased crime:* Need more be said concerning that?

•*Lovers of pleasure:* Hasn't the present day about reached the total fulfillment of *this* prophecy?

•*Wars and armaments:* Practically every household has been touched one time or another by the untold suffering of war. Statistics in this case can be disregarded, as the newspapers and television media give us more than an ample supply of evidence that this prophecy is actually being fulfilled in a more realistic way than ever before thought possible.

•*Masterful delusions:* In Matthew 24:4,5 there is a distinct warning that many shall come in the name of Christ, claiming to *be* Christ, and that many will be deceived by this "silent second coming." In verse 27, however, it states that, *"For as the lightning cometh out of the east, and shineth even unto the west, so shall also the coming of the Son of man be."*

•*The gospel to all the world:* This prophecy as told in Matthew 24:14 has just about been fulfilled. Practically all of humanity has become acquainted with Christianity through radio, television, printed word and word of mouth. Estimates place the complete fulfillment of this prediction within our lifetime. And it is when these predictions have come true that peace will control the world.

In Micah 4:3,4 it states, *"And he shall judge among many people and rebuke strong nations afar off; and they shall beat their swords into plowshares, and their spears into pruning hooks: nation shall not lift up a sword against nation, neither shall they learn war any more.*

"But they shall sit every man under his vine and under his fig tree; and none shall make them afraid: for the mouth of the Lord of hosts hath spoken of it."

Will there be peace in the world and in Vietnam, you ask? No, not according to the Bible. The wars and calamities we encounter are only a prelude to the beginning of what will eventually lead to ultimate peace, but this will not happen through human endeavors.

Miss D. G. of Grand Rapids, Michigan, is greatly distressed by certain predictions made for her and to her by an eminent astrologer and fortune-teller. She asks:

"Can I change the outcome of these predictions?"

First, allow me to clarify one point. No one really knows your future except God, and He will most certainly not inform you of it through a fortune-teller or an astrologer. The Calvinists believe that our destiny has been preordained and that whatever we do has already been decided for us from before the foundation of the world. There is no actual biblical evidence for this, and inasmuch as man was endowed with a free will, this in itself indicates that there is a flexibility in life and that we help determine the outcome of our future by our own actions.

When someone makes a prediction regarding your future, it is just that. A prediction—not a guaranteed prophecy—and it is subject to alterations, external influences and your own personal reaction to events that shape your life. It is similar to a computer that has a few basic facts at its disposal and then adds to these a number of "ifs" and a number of "presumptions."

If you like the prediction, fine, remember it. If you don't, simply reject the prediction and continue to choose the best of two possibilities whenever you are confronted with a destiny-shaping decision. You *can* work out your own future, but this of course is limited by your personal reaction to the workings of the forces of Good and Evil.

This psychic age has seen a rebirth of ancient rites and pagan practices, and witchcraft has made more inroads within the last few years than most of the others combined.

It is therefore understandable that Mrs. A. W. of Pensa-cola, Florida, should ask the following question:

"Do witches really exist in our modern day, and what do they do?"

There is no doubt that witchcraft has survived the wear and tear of the ages and is at present undergoing a total re-vamping, in order to make it acceptable to the masses.

Until 1951, laws against witchcraft and sorcery were still in existence in Great Britain, and death by hanging was a definite threat for anyone caught in the practice of the an-cient rites. It must have thrown terror into a number of people, but Sybil Leek, also known as the high priestess of Witchcraft, was not among them. In those years, Sybil lived in the New Forest area in England, but since her arrival in the United States, she has exercised a major influence on the growth and development of witchcraft in the United States and abroad.

Witchcraft and outright devil worship are closely related and constitute a decided threat to our Christian society. In Catholic Mexico two practitioners of witchcraft were lynched as recently as the 1950's and in many other places in the world—Russia, Lower Saxony, England—witch trials were held and convictions were handed down.

The Bible is vehemently opposed to witchcraft. Doctrines of this "religion" include devil worship, demonic fantasies, demonic possession, heresy, anti-God teachings, indulging in insatiable carnal lusts (sex orgies) and astral projection for evil purposes.

There is nothing to indicate that present-day witchcraft advocates have adopted a new set of rules or doctrines. It is the mysterious quality and the supernatural aspect of the ancient rites of witchcraft that hold true fascination for the thousands of new converts.

Undoubtedly confused and worried by the often erratic behavior of the present new generation, the following writer asks for help in understanding what really lies behind all this.

Mrs. D. L. of Kansas City, Kansas, asks:

"Why does today's youth feel they need their shabby dress, long hair, drugs and the like? How will their behavior affect our future society inasmuch as they are the ones to lead the nation thirty years from now?"

I am glad someone asked, for I am one of millions no doubt who have often wondered about the same thing. Singling out one of the bearded ones for a talk session, I cornered him and kept forcing the questions on him until he came up with some answers.

"Why the long hair, the 'sexless' look?" he asked. "I'll tell you why. Most of us reject the earlier ideas of manhood. My dad, my uncle, my brothers, they all say, 'Keep shaved so you look like a real man,' so I do, and know what? All the homosexuals are clean-shaven and suddenly I feel that perhaps I don't want to be a clean-shaven smelly polished young man. I want to be a *man.* I'm sure the first hippie felt that way, and he grew a beard like his grandfather and great-grandfather did, and it made him feel good. I reacted that way and grew mine. Long hair was next in line. Ever seen ferocious pirates, medieval knights pictured as well-groomed, well-trimmed men? They were men and looked like it, so again we—and I mean most of us—wear beards *and* long hair. *It is identification we are after.* To top this, many like to be identified with someone else, not themselves, so they act and dress like the others in the group.

Soon we felt like outcasts and formed communes—and that's where the real 'us' can be found. Communes are for the idea of getting back to the land. In our opinion technology has made us animals again, so we want to get back to the land, start over again and relive life the way early man did, tending his own flocks, raising his own family and growing his own vegetables."

"How about the drugs?" I interrupted.

"That's the fault of the older generation. We need examples. We need heroes to identify with. But *our* heroes, our fathers and mothers, gave us a supreme example by inhaling nicotine by the pack, drinking whiskey by the gallon (at 'social gatherings' only, they like to point out) and abuse the privilege of buying medicinal drugs without prescription at the corner drugstore. They had their booze, their cigarettes, and the like but still told us, 'Don't do as we do, do as we say.' But how can you work that logic on a child?

"Believe me, we are no more drugged than our parents, we are more open about it. We were already drugged before we came into the world, through *their* alcohol, *their* sleeping pills, *their* tranquilizers and *their* cigarettes. We were conditioned to the use of drugs before we saw the first light of day—so why not use some drugs as pacifiers when we grow up?

"I am convinced that our experiences are much like those of our parents, but we expose our emotions to public scrutiny. They didn't. And like them, we'll pull out of this mania. Already drugs are losing their charm; suddenly LSD looks more frightening than ever. As to the love-beads—why have the beads if you can have the real thing?"

Now as to the basic part of Mrs. D. L.'s question, "Will their behavior affect our future society," the answer is an emphatic *no*. We are not going to have an oncoming generation of morons and deformities, because the youth are beginning to realize their true role in life. Mind me, I am not saying that *all* of them will turn at the right time. It will be the minority of this new generation that will rule this nation; the majority will be either indifferent or cooperative. We will evolve into a system where the minority will rule the majority, with great benevolence, at least that's the way they will look at it.

There is an interesting thing that fascinates me about this generation. They are trying to escape *to* something instead of *from* something. There is something positive about them. This generation no doubt is going to be a generation of intellectuals, abhorring pornographic material because within the next year or so there won't be any need for it. They're going to realize that God made their bodies; that human bodies are beautiful, and that they weren't made to be abused. They are going to put sex in its proper perspective. Nobody has abused sex more than the present grown-up generation has done. The parents of the new generation (*our* age bracket!) had their sex clubs; overt sex activities behind the curtains, bushes and closed doors, in the old buggy seat, in the barn and in the rumble seat. Let's be honest. This new generation is not doing anything the previous generation left out. They're just more honest and open about it. They've stopped the trend of hypocrisy.

Don't worry about their future. They'll straighten out and come 'round. It's *their* future that's at stake. Not ours.

I always feel flattered when people ask my opinion regarding religion, convictions, etc., but even though I am quite taken with my own opinion, I don't want to create the impression that mine is the only valid one.

Such is the case with the question I received from Miss F. H. from Baton Rouge, Louisiana.

"Is there a way to pray and be sure you get what you want?"

Do I wish there were! I'd be the first one to exploit it, for it would eliminate my own problems once and for all! But all kidding aside, I regard prayer as a form of "mental telepathy." In praying you are transferring, visualizing, your conscious desires to One Whom you consider more powerful than you and asking Him to work in your behalf. Now, considering that you *are* directing your conscious magnetic energy impulses toward God, you must bear in mind that you ought not to pray recklessly. Don't ask for the impossible. Ask for the possible, bearing in mind the *promises* regarding truthful honest prayer as listed in the Bible. If plants can communicate (and this fact is proven by researcher Cleve Backster of the Backster Research Foundation in New York) then it is reasonable to assume that the Higher Power that created all of us can also communicate with His creation. Prayer is that channel of communication, and interestingly enough, the more you "practice" prayer, the more results you will get, for conscious serious prayer clears the channel to God and makes your prayer more forceful.

No, there is no sure-fire formula for prayer, except the one *you* find for yourself after working at keeping the "channel" open. Look into your own heart. Do you *really want* and *need* everything you ever prayed for? Aren't you glad many of your requests *weren't* answered?

CHAPTER EIGHT

Compared to other year endings in history, the transition of 1970 into 1971 has been rather on the peaceful side. Yet, in the eyes of the future historians it may well be regarded as one of the most significant milestones in the development of this planet.

For many long years now, my probing psychic sense has brought me a new awareness of the laws of cause and effect. The Golden Rule, as others call it, often creates blessings beyond measure when followed; but when transgressed it breeds overtones of wars, terrifying tension and inventions that take us to (and over) the threshold of Armageddon.

Predictions have been given throughout history, and humanity has always reacted. The psychic's role and responsibility in this is great. There is nothing more terrifying than to hold a key that can unlock the window of the future. It is far from comforting to realize that one major prediction can spark a chain reaction of information and rumors, and that because of this, many people feel forced to alter the course of their lives.

In the course of the next thirty years, I see three distinct periods of development. The first period starts with a renewed threat to the United States mainland by Communist Cuba and ends with the government-sponsored "Mind-Shaping Program" of 1979. The period from 1980 to 1990 will be equally as important as it will deal with "Space Migration" and the "Invisibility of Man." The last ten-year period, leading to the year 2000, will bring both blessings and wars.

These events have already cast their shadow; I am merely pulling them into focus with the hope that by reading and listening to them, we may learn to recognize the signs leading up to these developments. Many of them we may be able to avoid. Others we will experience or merely observe. This is sure—no period in history will bear any resemblance to the time ahead.

PERIOD ONE: 1971-1979

Cuba Poses New Threat to the United States

I get the distinct impression that the United States is headed exactly for a destination charted for it by the U.S.S.R. While being engaged in Southeast Asia and the Middle East, our government will be lulled to sleep in regard to the possibility of a new Cuban threat to our security. Great fear will spread throughout the eastern states because of a new buildup of Soviet missiles in Cuba. I see top-secret reports being relayed to the President, informing him of the missile buildup. I see him practically unable to act. Every one of the missile sites is manned by Russian personnel. Every one of them is aimed at a specific American target. I also see a cable deep in the water right off the Florida coast. It is a rather thin cable, but I see it connected to Cuba. It carries within it much death and pain.

Students Organizing Killer Squads

Before the year 1975, student rebellion on college campuses will take another turn and operate along new and different lines. Instead of developing mass unrest, disturbances, race and social riots, the hard-core militant students will develop carefully planned assassinations of high-ranking officials as well as sabotage programs aimed at destroying the nation's communications centers, power plants, dams, bridges and refineries. Formed into small operational units, these killer squads will be highly trained in the use of explosives by some of them now undergoing training outside the United States.

While these destruction squads are in operation, their leaders will promote goodwill and cooperation on the nation's campuses so as to mislead the masses.

Migration from the United States

Within the next four years, many people who would never have envisioned themselves parting from their beloved country will feel forced to leave the United States to escape the violence and destruction which by that time will seem almost inevitable.

Mexico, Brazil and Sweden will become some of the more sought-after countries of refuge for these migrants. Others, who for family reasons cannot leave the continental United States, will in fact construct hideouts in the rocks and mountains of the interior of the United States.

Complete Energy Breakthrough

During the 1970's, science will begin to discover that every element of energy has more to it than just a negative and a positive side. It will discover properties that are more far reaching, owing to the minute examination of a particle thus far ignored. It will be this discovery which will be of prime importance in the America of the future.

In conjunction with this will come a new concept that teaches that the energy forces within humans *also* have more properties than previously expected and that these forces are directly responsible for man's so-called gifts and talents.

Based on the knowledge gained from these properties, tests, technical data and behavioral patterns will be established, which will be used to program individual educational workloads to enable each person to become a better and more productive member of his community. Together with the knowledge and understanding of these properties, however, will come the danger of knowing how to organize and control them in others, making mind control within reach of many scientists.

Possessing an acute awareness of the exact weaknesses of the human mind will enable man to construct electronic equipment that will be used to influence thought patterns and control jealousies, pride, hate, joy and other emotions. This knowledge will also be used to amplify an individual's talents, such as music, science and business, vastly increasing the number of geniuses in the country.

Earthquake in the Making

With my mind's eye, I have seen a large and very destructive earthquake take place in what I identify as the Middle

East, some time before 1976. It will cause a number of minor yet also destructive tremors in the United States and in Western Europe. Water will play a dramatic role in this terrible calamity, and many people will die as a result of the tremendous floods that will destroy heavily populated areas.

The force of the quake will damage some major dams in the United States and affect their power output. As a result certain segments of industry will suffer greatly.

Indians Honored Citizens

In this decade, much attention will be focused on the American Indian and his honored place in our society. He will arise as a national figure and will represent a symbol of survival and physical fitness. Indian culture will once again begin to bloom. Certain educational programs will be patterned after Indian traditions.

A Return of Prohibition

As if to make up for the ill effects of pollution, a nationwide physical-fitness program will sweep the country during the last part of the present decade. Though not actually outlawed, alcohol will be regarded as a force of destruction.

Social drinking will become as extinct as it was in the days of Prohibition. Medical proof will be provided to demonstrate that alcohol not only affects the human brain and body, but that it has a far-reaching effect on future generations.

Genocide in the Americas

Some time before the end of the seventies, a shocking tribal genocide will be revealed. The method of mass murder employed will be far more cruel, though not as extensive, than any of the methods used on the Jewish people during the extermination process of the Second World War, but some of the same people who shaped that program will also guide this one.

The mass murders will bear strong resemblances to the crimes committed against the American Indians in the early years of our country. These to-be-announced genocides will take place around certain heavily populated areas in South America.

Mining Will Be Different

It may be hard to believe and the labor unions most certainly won't agree to it, but a new invention to be made around the middle of this decade will make it possible to draw minerals from the earth electronically. Physically extracting the raw minerals and coal from the earth will be obsolete. Metals gained this new way will be purer than those extracted today.

Another advantage of this new "extraction method" will be that it will lead to the discovery of at least three new metals and several minerals never before known. These discoveries in turn will introduce a new and higher standard of living in this country.

Communist Infiltration Made Public

Within the near future facts will come to the surface proving that some of the men who attempted to thwart President Nixon's plans to go into Cambodia are Communist-inspired and propagandists of the Red Chinese Communist philosophy. Many of these people have been planted in various branches of the government by old-time Communists. In the past their recruiting was done in and through universities and other schools for higher education. Now their emphasis has changed to the junior generation and the older dissatisfied government employees.

Noah's Ark To Be Discovered

Much has been said in recent years about the reported discovery of Noah's Ark, and even though pieces of wood have been found on Mount Ararat, these pieces are not part of the ancient ark.

I do believe that the pieces found are part of a large structure, predating the Deluge, and that they floated on the waters of the Flood and were stranded on the slopes of Mount Ararat.

When discovered, the Ark will be found on a higher elevation on the same mountain. Its discovery will cause great controversy between science and religion, for it will not look like an oceangoing vessel but bear more resemblance to a sturdy tugboat. It will be clear that it was designed to float. It will look somewhat like a natural formation—part of the mountain on which it is found—but the discovery of an almost limitless number of rooms within it will do away with that idea.

When observing the group that is going to find the Ark, I see no foreigners in its leadership but only nationals from the country in which it is found. American money will make it possible for these Turkish scientists to complete the long search for the ship.

I also see a tunnel, a cave, being dug into the side of the mountain in order to be able to examine the Ark from beneath.

There are two names closely connected with the discovery. I only see the initials "L" and "M." I also have seen a tremendously violent storm hit the site of the discovery.

Most of the activities connected with this will take place within the next thirty-six months.

New Breakthrough in Medicine

Within a relatively short time, a great new breakthrough is going to cause much commotion in the medical world, and will prove to be of far-reaching significance in the field of organ transplants.

Thus far experiments made in transplanting parts of human bodies have not been completely satisfactory. The new method to be followed will be the implantation of newly developed artificial organs to take over the function of the kidneys and the heart. These electrically powered units will be placed within the body permanently and will be powered by a new source of energy that will be found in the human blood. The amount of this chemical prevalent in one single drop of blood will power the new devices for several months.

Laser Gun

A destructive new weapon developed from the laser ray will be introduced in this decade and will outperform all other weapons in deadly accuracy. Not only will it be possible to use this ray as a "stunner," but it will eventually become possible to control the weapon by thought-action. One laser gun placed strategically (satellites?) can hold an entire nation at bay. It is this weapon that will determine the outcome of the Sino-American War of the 1990's.

Assassination Attempt on Nixon

Before the end of his present term, an assassination attempt will be made on the life of President Nixon, but he will survive.

The would-be assassin, a middle-aged man with a shock of brown hair, built rather slightly, and with an occasional twitch of his right shoulder, will attack the President while he is appearing before a gathering of people. I cannot see the name of the man, nor can I at this time pinpoint the exact location. One or possibly two of the President's bodyguards will be relieved of their assignment because of this incident.

I have attempted to identify the type of weapon used, but it is obscure. Where the President is standing I do see blood seeping to the ground. It seems to be coming from a wound somewhere near or on one of his legs.

This assassination attempt will be used as cause for a complete revamping of the United States Secret Service.

Exhaust Fumes Controlled

Within a short time auto exhaust fumes will be controlled by means of a new sort of muffler that will change the poisonous gases now spewed from the engine's exhaust into a harmless gas and release it into the atmosphere without injury to the human race.

The man who will perfect this muffler is a genius without much formal education. He will derive most of his abilities from his psychic power. He will claim that this invention has come to him through his contacts with some of the greatest minds of the past. Although I do not know his complete name, I do see that the first letter in his last name is found among the first five letters of the alphabet.

Signs of Ancient Civilization

Two objects, closely resembling flagpoles with a heavy knob on top, will emerge out of the waters off the southeast coast of the United States and will introduce the world to a new, hitherto unknown civilization. I don't see the significance of these objects but I do see them connected to a great ship beneath. I see the entire object "pop up" from the ocean bottom as if its own buoyancy had forced it up. The ship is filled with artifacts that will enable us to determine its age and the importance of the civilization that built it.

The result of the investigation will turn out to be more than just an archaeological controversy. It will cause the archaeologists and geologists to revamp their most basic theories.

Rising of the Southern States

In the future, beginning with the year 1974, the United States will find itself looking to the South in almost every area of endeavor.

The people of the South will be directly responsible for this. Through the many social revolutions of the 1950's and 1960's, they have manifested a strong self-discipline. Their fundamental religious beliefs have kept them from inciting the bloody riots that have plagued the northern cities (Watts, Detroit, Newark). They have been slow to anger in comparison with the North, but relatively quick in their reaction to proven injustices.

As a result, industry, education and culture will make great strides in southern states such as Tennessee, Alabama, Mississippi, Arkansas and Georgia. Creativity as never seen before will also draw many artists and scholars to the South so they can practice their profession in an atmosphere of frontierism and freedom from forced traditions.

Important legislation and leadership in all areas of federal government will come from southern leaders, who have been waiting for this development for years. They have been patiently preparing themselves for their role in national government.

Many of the so-called "sleepy" cities of the South will become magnificent metropolises of greatness and responsibility. They will no longer be led, but will *lead*.

It will mark the beginning of a *new* South.

Portable Atomic Reactors

What has been a dream for many years is now entering the final stages. Portable atomic reactors, powerful enough to be used where gasoline engines now play their most prominent role, are on the drawing board. These power plants will still take several years before they get into actual mass production, but the principle of atomic fission can now be adequately controlled so as not to cause any danger.

The public is not aware of this, but shortly certain merchant ships will begin using a prototype of this new reactor, and based on the resulting reports, small atomic reactors for planes, automobiles and trains will be developed. This will go hand in hand with a dismantling of all conventional industrial power plants. Atomic power will take over in industry and transportation. Pessimistic studies predicting a decline of the role of atomic power will be proven to have been wrong.

Crack in North Pole

A disturbing development in the earth's crust at the North Pole has been forcing itself into my mind. It is a crack—several hundred feet in width—that is appearing at the North Pole, forcing itself down for hundreds of miles along a straight line until it branches off in another direction and takes on the shape of the letter "Y." Several major cities are demolished while the tear continues. Looking closer, I have seen one of the African nations receiving most of the damage—why, I don't know. I can see the crack clearly, but the countries through which it will pass are still as in a haze. This natural tragedy will have a definite effect on the location of the poles. There may be climatological changes as a result, for I see an orange all covered with a thick white coat of frost. Perhaps this means that some of our tropical and subtropical areas of the world will undergo a complete change in climate.

Timing of this event is difficult to get.

Life in Outer Space

Within the next sixty months, we will discover that a highly developed form of life exists in outer space and *has* existed there for a long time. I don't know the names of the planets involved, but I have seen this extraterrestrial life and know that we will find facts that will verify this. Contrary to expectations, this discovery will not be the result of an interplanetary flight but will be based on a scientific study conducted on something that will hit our earth from space. Coupled to this will be a further study of the origin of the moon that will reveal facts so shocking that we will think twice before venturing any *further* into the deep blackness of space.

The United States will play a minor role in these discoveries, England and Russia will be in the lead position. Someone whose name begins with the letter "U" will play a significant role in this. I get the feeling that some of these civilizations in outer space are aware of what is happening on this planet, and I have received strong vibrations of their past presence here on earth.

Cure For Cancer?

A new ray of light in the fight to gain control of cancer is beginning to appear. A team of medical researchers in the southern part of the United States will discover what appears to be a basic cure for cancer. A fungus that can be found in some of the southern states will yield a substance that is the active agent. I feel that it has already been extremely effective in combating cancer in rats.

Application of this new substance to human test cases is but a matter of time.

New Approach to Healing

Toward the end of the 1970's many medical doctors will join the ranks of the faith healers, and as a result new healing methods will be introduced in the medical world.

What is now known as "spiritual healing" and "faith healing" will be channeled into one of the greatest revolutionary changes in the history of mankind. It will force the entire field of conventional medicine to revert to hitherto unaccepted healing methods. Medical doctors of the late seventies will begin to accept faith healing and will try to practice its principles wherever possible. The doctor of the twenty-first century will eventually end up knowing more about physics, energies and electronic substances than the chemistry of medicine. A new type of chemistry, known as the chemistry of energy, will replace the then outdated chemistry of today.

Specialists of that century will also be specialists at healing from a distance. Patients will no longer have to see their doctor for a physical examination. Thought transmissions will enable the physician to pick up the patient's subconscious problems, and this will enable him to diagnose the illness.

Mind-Shaping Program in the Making

Dissatisfied with public political thinking, careful consideration is now being given to a mental health program that will, when finally enacted, be as revolutionary to human development as was the wheel to transportation.

Between the years 1979 and 1982, this plan will go into action and will completely reshape the system governing the nation's public health. Mental programs for the future will be geared to political action rather than to the free will of the individual. Absolute standards will be formulated as to what constitutes good and healthy thinking, and these nationwide standards will be enforced through specially created legal bodies, somewhat different from our present court system. There will be no direct limitation imposed on active thought, but unless individuals channel their thoughts in a direction that is in line with governing political trends and realities, the "thought courts" will intervene and the "sick" mind will be subject to "modified thought," or as we know it today, brainwashing.

Psychiatrists and psychologists will no longer be able to enjoy the freedom of movement and action they have today. All specialists dealing and working with the human mind will act under the government health standard and will function as civil servants. There will be a politically oriented "healing treatment" reserved for special cases. This treatment will be an absolute brainwashing, for the "enemies of the state only."

During this time, individual thought impressions as well as the fingerprints of United States citizens will be coded and stored in master files.

The movement that will bring our country to this unexpected development will be spearheaded by the reactionary generation of today.

PERIOD TWO: 1980–1990

A Change in Love Imminent

Love as it is known today will cease to exist before the end of this century. Man will retain his ability to love, but it will become more a mechanical function, because the ability to *love* is an essential part of our ability to *think*, and this will slowly be curtailed.

Within a relatively short time—but certainly before 1985 —children will be given mandatory psychological and physical tests soon after birth to determine their capabilities and abilities. Their programmed future will be based on the outcome of these tests.

At this point, political action programs will be designed for each child, and his entire life will be guided by the programmed future determined for him by the computer. Undesirable tendencies discovered in his early years will be corrected along standardized lines prescribed by the federal government. Children will know their parents, but will consider them items of necessity rather than persons of compassion and greatness.

Standardized types of love and affection will prevail, and no deviation from these norms will be tolerated.

Sharp Increase in Energy Communication

Because of the physiological and emotional changes now developing within the human body, a new awareness of psychic phenomena will come to the surface. People will become more *intuitive*, more *clairvoyant*, more *clairaudiant* and more *sensitive* in all areas of energy communication.

By the year 1980 intuition and clairvoyance will in some ways become as much a part of people's lives as the telephones now hanging on the walls of their homes. My ability will no longer be regarded as something unusual, and the use of psychic power will be widespread and greatly accepted.

Along with its growing usefulness, this gift will be misused by many. There will be those who, gifted as they are, will use their clairvoyancy for exploitation. Many will use it commercially or to control others. It will place too much power in the hands of a ruthless few who, owing to their highly developed psychic sense, will form a group that will eventually rule this nation with what amounts to dictatorial power.

Racial Purification Program

During the early 1980's there will be a new aggressive segregation program introduced in our legislature, aimed at purifying the races so that blacks will become blacker and whites whiter.

There will be three definite programs; one for blacks, one for whites and one for the yellow inhabitants of the United States. Great agony will accompany this purification plan, more for the Jewish part of our population than for any other ethnic group. Leaders among them will use this as an excuse to purify *their* race from all who have joined their faith through marriage with outsiders.

Tall People

People in the United States will be of taller stature than in the past. This increase in size will continue until it takes on grotesque proportions.

The basic reason for the rapid and elevated growth process is built into our food supply. Huge quantities of chemicals, drugs and antibiotics consumed by the present generation will be a direct cause. For example, chemicals used in rapid-growth formulae for poultry are in turn collected in the human system through consumption of these birds. Notwithstanding contrary scientific opinion, these chemicals will definitely have a detrimental effect on people, for along with the rapid and accelerated growth will come a magnified weakness of personality and body.

Space Migration—War on Moon

I see that shortly before the middle of the 1980's, immigrants from the United States and Russia will attempt to colonize and develop the moon. By that time, man's space travel will have become rather luxurious. The new generation of spaceships will be guided along their paths by invisible rays, reminiscent of laser beams.

This planned migration will eventually result in "police actions" on the moon between Russian and American armed men, for both will want to secure the strategic areas of the moon for operational reasons. I see death and blood spilled on the surface of the moon, but at the same time the same death seems to reach down and touch the earth and cause much physical destruction and mental anguish here.

While concentrating on the moon colonization program, I received impressions that the summer of 1972 may go down in history as a major milestone in the space exploration program. I see the number of thirteen or fourteen, which I believe is the number of space units involved in the activities that will capture the headlines that summer. These spaceships will be engaged at that time in a program that will be more adventurous than scientific. Two men—one whose name begins with "W" and one whose name begins with "A"—will be the men guiding this project.

I do not see whether this is a Russian or American space venture.

Change in Printing Methods

The printed word will always exist as one of the most effective methods of communication, but looking ahead, I see that printing processes will change so abruptly and drastically that it will be hard to keep with the sudden improvements.

If present discoveries are pursued diligently, the printing of the middle 1980's will be done according to the "instant transfer process." In this process there will be no plates, ink, rollers or presses. Instead the transfer will be done electronically and the results will be so superb that it will seem as if we have entered an entirely new age. Entire sections of newspapers and magazines will be three-dimensional in form.

Looking at a printed page produced in the middle 1980's will remind one of the old silent movies. The new printed page will have everything but sound.

Under this new method of reproduction, a single master copy fed into a duplicating machine will give birth to an unlimited number of multidimensional copies. The rate of reproduction will be fantastic, the expenses almost nothing. Instead of paper, plastic will be used as the basic ingredient.

New Human Species to Appear

An unbelievable, yet very real, human species will soon make its appearance on the world scene, starting in the laboratories in the United States. Not only will this species be developed completely outside the mother's womb, but it will become a superior species owing to the scientific "shaping" process that will guide existence.

The child of that special breed will have nothing to say about his own future. The lessons learned in selective breeding of animals will be of great value for the perfection of the new humans. Unknown to most people in the United States, this selective-breeding process controlled and carried out in a completely germ-free chamber outside the mother's body has already passed the initial testing stage and is being brought into full operation in a laboratory of one of the major chemical firms in the western part of the country.

Era of the Unspoken Word

Transforming thoughts into images *at will* on a TV-like screen will be a reality around the middle 1980's, although prototypes will be in use a few years prior to that by one of our three-letter intelligence agencies.

This new device will introduce great changes within the investigative arm of the judiciary. Starting in 1984, criminals will no longer be subject to the polygraph test, but will be required to undergo the "mental image" test.

The telephone system of that time, too, will undergo fascinating changes and will no longer transfer sound impulses along its whispering wires. It will be used for thought-transmission impulses. The greatest use of thought transmission, however, will be in the field of mental health. It will enable psychiatrists—who by that time will be under state control—to study a patient's mental problems and thought patterns as they develop.

It will also—and this will be more regrettable—introduce the danger of "thought espionage" into our society.

Healing Centers—Concentration Camps?

By the year 1987, "healing centers" will have been established throughout this country and throughout most other civilized nations. These centers of forced tranquillity will actually be a series of highly advanced concentration camps where political prisoners will be housed for the duration of their "mental purification treatment."

Because of the many dangers threatening Western civilization in the middle 1980's, anyone who has destructive tendencies or is a known advocate of a different system of government, endangering the iron-grip control of the Establishment, will be placed in these correction centers.

These centers will not be known as concentration camps, but will be called mental healing centers when legislation governing their existence is introduced into the House in late 1984. The Department of Health, Education and Welfare will be responsible for their operation.

Thought Machine Under Development

For some time now I have been aware of specialized and classified research being conducted somewhere in the central United States, aimed at developing a "TAD" machine—a development that has often been mentioned as a vague possibility in science-fiction literature.

This "Thought-Action-Deed" machine will be an electronic instrument that will enable the owner to tune in electronically to past, present and future events based on computer analysis of the pattern of history.

This machine will first make its entry in 1986. Access to the first prototype, however, will be limited to the scientists directly involved and to particular key members of the executive branch of the government. During the first ten years of its existence there will be no public involvement or utilization of this device, but the year 1996 will mark the moment of change. In that year it will be released for mass production.

TAD will operate on the theory that thoughts are actual energy and that since true energy cannot be destroyed, words and thoughts of the past continue to linger on through the ages. TAD will locate, separate and amplify these out of the ether and make them audible. At first, the device will be limited to working with words that actually have been *spoken.* This is because their frequencies will be much more intense, as they are made up of a combination of mental impulse and physical reaction. How far TAD will ultimately go in retrieving information I cannot say, but I do get the impression that a range of two thousand years will not be impossible.

The first major improvement on this device will make its entry about 1992. From that year on TAD will be able to pick up, record and amplify impressions of human *thought* as well. This development will be followed by a third phase, some years later, that of bringing in the accompanying video vibrations, so that we will have both audio and video of the past as well as the present.

Ultimately—and I see this for the late 1990's—there will be no privacy of thought left. Whatever thought is conceived from then on, whatever deed enacted or word said, will be open for public inspection and can and *will* be viewed and heard by those who use TAD.

PERIOD THREE: 1991–2000

Increased Respect For the Bible

Through new archaeological finds in the Middle East and the countries of the Near East, the Bible will gain greatly in stature. By 1996 most of the historical references given in the Bible will have been substantiated. More than ever before, it will become a guideline. Many of the Western nations will revamp their systems of government to bring them in harmony with what they consider biblical guidelines.

Thorough study will reveal that the Bible is far ahead of present discoveries in the field of science and psychology. Many spiritual giants will use it to unlock the doors to thus far hidden powers. Entirely new scientific discoveries will be made because of new understanding of Bible facts.

I see new facts coming to light, pinpointing the exact location of the biblical Ark of the Covenant, containing the Ten Commandments written on tables of stone.

Invisibility of Man

During the late nineties, American and Russian scientists will have succeeded in perfecting a device enabling man to become invisible to the naked eye.

The exact shape of the crucial component of this device is not exactly clear to me at this moment, but I see two images —one resembling a flashlight with a big round head, the other bearing the likeness of an aerosol can.

As of now, the Russians are leading in this project, but I see Western scientists closing in on them. Because of its close resemblance to pure science-fiction, neither the Russians nor the Western scientists involved want any publicity.

The device will not be injurious to man, but because of its high cost and uncontrollability its use will be extremely limited, if used at all.

Strict Sunday Laws in Planning Stage

Irrefutable evidence is now rising to the surface indicating that our nation is heading for a climactic period in its history.

I predict that by 1983, the long-treasured doctrine of separation between church and state will have disappeared. The state will enter into the ecumenical fusion of the churches and will support the majority of Protestant religions. This support will include rigorous enforcement of a new series of Sunday laws, regulating activities allowed on Sunday. A bill authorizing calendar reform will also be passed.

Many seers and sensitives have gone on record predicting the approach of the coming of the Antichrist. I predict these new Sunday laws will be the first of his treacheries and his first official intrusions on the liberty to worship as guaranteed by the United States Constitution.

The forthcoming battle between the state and the remnant church (those who do not comply with the new calendar-reform regulations) had its birth in the dawn of human history. The Antichrist, most theologians agree, will be a being, a force, striving to create events and affect history in such a way that religious freedom will be drastically curtailed. The day of rest, the basic fundamental doctrine of all of Christianity, will be caught in the tightening vise of a renewed surge of paganism.

The Fourth Commandment, which governs the rest day of God's creation, has always been the nucleus of every known Christian religious movement. Since the moment Israel was given a day of rest to commemorate the completion of the process of creation—the birthday of creation—this day has tied the Jewish nation together as no other command. It was God's stamp upon the Jewish race to identify them as His own amidst the heathen tribes of the Middle East and show that they were the "elect," the nation chosen by God.

It is therefore obvious that the destruction of organized religion will be greatly enhanced by the eradication of the significance of this day, for one way or another most religions have adopted the day of rest as either on the seventh or the first day of the week. *If the antichristian movement is to become successful, it must upset the weekly cycle but accomplish this in such a way that all religion will become dependent upon this new day of rest, as dictated by the new world calendar.*

There are two basic questions underlying the entire doctrine of a weekly rest period. 1) Has the weekly cycle remained constant from the time of creation, and *if* a day was lost, have corrective measures been taken to rectify this? and 2) What is the position of the seventh day of rest versus the first day of the week? Both of these questions are fundamental to the problem, for upon them hangs the decision of whether to agree with calendar reformists.

Referring to the first question, Bible scholars adhere to the unwavering position that the Jews throughout the centuries have observed the seventh day of the weekly cycle uninterruptedly. When the Israelites were roaming the desert for forty years, God reemphasized the value of the day by supplying twice as much manna for their sustenance on Friday, but none on the day following, since it was their day of rest. It received sanction again when the Ten Commandments were issued. Then came Christ, and as the Lord of Creation, He again sanctified the day instituted in paradise as the birthday of creation.

The great change from seventh-day observance to first-day observance came not as a result of a new biblical teaching but as the outcome of human interference in nonhuman affairs. The validity of the seven-day cycle was never questioned, nor was there any real doubt as to whether the cycle remained the same and is still as sacred as when it was first given.

Chief Justice Clark, speaking for the Supreme Court of

North Carolina concerning the origin of Sunday-keeping, said:

"Sunday was first adopted by Christians in lieu of Saturday long years after Christ, in commemoration of the Resurrection. The first 'Sunday law' was enacted in the year 321 after Christ, soon after the emperor Constantine had abjured paganism, and apparently for a different reason than the Christian observance of the day. . . . Evidently Constantine was still something of a heathen. As late as the year 409 two rescripts of the emperors Honorius and Theodosius indicate that Christians then generally observed the Sabbath [Saturday, not Sunday].

The curious may find these set out in full, Codex Just., lib. I, tit. IX, Cx 13. Not till near the end of the ninth century was Sunday substituted by law for Saturday as the day of rest by a decree of the emperor Leo (Leo Cons., 54)."

From that time on, the Sunday observance was rigidly enforced, and even though many groups held on to the seventh-day observance, organized Christianity changed its day of worship and eliminated God's appointed day.

The measures taken have been drastic, even to the point of demanding the death penalty for those who choose to ignore the papal ruling, but the week as a seven-day unit is still intact. The matter might have rested here had it not been for the prophecy found in Daniel 7:25. Speaking about a new kingdom that was to come forth out of ten kingdoms that ruled Europe after the breakup of the Roman Empire, Daniel said, *"And he shall speak great words against the most High and shall wear out the saints of the most High, and think to change times and laws."* What has not been completed in the time of the Roman Empire will no doubt take place during the rule of the antichristian movement, which will commence when the ecumenical ideologists water down Christianity to make it conform to the desires of the business world.

Orthodox Christianity will be dealt a death blow when the Sunday observance becomes law, coupled with a general calendar reform based on months of an equal number of days. Jews and orthodox Christians will lose their regularly recurring Sabbath; Mohammedans will lose their Friday and more liberal Christians who do not want to subscribe to the calendar reform will nevertheless lose their Sunday. While business will undoubtedly reap tremendous profits because of the advantage of regularity, religion will suffer greatly.

When the Sunday law is finally enacted—with or without calendar reform—it will mark the end of an era and will signify the grand entry of the antichristian movement. As far back as 1889, steps were taken in the United States to insure the inclusion of a Sunday law in the Constitution. The Reverend M. A. Gault, in a letter dated June 3, 1889, and quoted by W. A. Blakely in *American State Papers,* p. 238, states, "We propose to incorporate in our national Constitution the moral and religious command, 'In it, [Sunday] thou shalt do no work,' except the works of necessity, and by external force of sheriffs we propose to arrest and punish all violators of this law." Prior to that, Dr. H. W. O. Millington reported in *Christian Statesman* of May 21, 1885, saying, "We may not be able to control the weather, but we are going to control Congress in reference to the securing of a Sunday Law for the District of Columbia."

I predict that new and more stringent Sunday observance laws are on their way.

Astral Projection

The practice of what has been called man's energy force leaving his body during sleep will be accepted as most common around the end of this century. It is an occult practice that was used in ancient days, and owing to the tremendous emphasis placed on psychic phenomena, it will be revived.

Man will again harness this power to the extent that he will be able to keep his physical body in a perfect state of existence with all its functions operating normally, while his intellect journeys off to faraway places, collecting information or conducting business. After completion, I see the energy force return to the body and inhabit it once again, *retaining* all information collected on its astral trip.

Use of Electronic Substance

I see a great effort being conducted when we near the year 2000 to duplicate many facets of Creation, and in some ways, man will be able to do so under the guidance of a new spiritual leader, who will emerge and take full control of those who wish to be "enlightened."

The story of the feeding of the five thousand, as related in the Bible will by then become an ordinary everyday occurrence, for by that time, man will be able to project from his consciousness an image of that which he desires and produce it through the thought process called "Electronic Substance."

The era of "thought creation," manufacturing substances with physical properties by thought *alone*, will bring man to a new level of mental development.

EPILOGUE

A great many times during the past few months I have experienced fleeting moments of worry and hesitation about the very basic concept of this book. Ofttimes facts and experiences needed for illustration of certain points could not be used for fear of betraying a confidence; on other occasions the names of some well-known national personalities had to be omitted for obvious reasons.

These were moments of crisis, yet the conviction that I had to share my knowledge of the "unknown" always justified the solution—and I continued to cooperate.

I believe that the accelerated interest in psychic phenomena we are now experiencing is something that has been preordained in the course of history. The world has known hundreds of prophets, seers and psychics during its six thousand years of human occupation. Now, however, we have reached a period marked by convulsive climaxes and controversies, and human frailty needs superhuman help. Acknowledgment of this need and the consequent development of the inherent psychic resources are the first steps to an escape back into a sane and just world.

I often drift back into my early years, and recall my boyhood experiences, "feeling" my first psychic encounter, and "touching" for the first time in my life the reality of the unseen and unfathomable world. The impression it left on me was tremendous.

That first encounter has left its mark and has made me cognizant of the realities of *real* life. Only now I feel awed instead of frightened. The bewilderment of it is still with me, but even though the weight of its responsibility has increased immensely over the years, it has made me grow, and I have learned how to *accept* it. For a psychic, simple acceptance is perhaps the hardest thing to learn.

Being psychic carries with it the responsibility of "knowing," and this makes the life of a professional psychic an unhappy one in many ways. With a developed psychic sense comes the knowledge not only of a deeper understanding of life, but of what lies beyond tomorrow and its tomorrow, which we may never see.

One does not need to be a pessimist to recognize that we are at present passing through one of the dark ages of this world's history. Nations are angry, and amidst the ceasefires that fringe the burning battlefields, new plots are hatched, new coups prepared. And all is recorded aforehand in the annals of pending history, for whatever happens, it casts a glimmer of itself ahead.

The psychic knows this and can prepare himself to gain a deeper understanding of life, of relationships. Having insight enables him to find his own personal place amidst the smoldering heat of the present where history fights with the future; where yesterdays change over into tomorrows and transform old loves to mere cold statistics. Being psychic can do much for the individual, if done nonprofessionally.

By just being psychic, one *receives*. By becoming a professional in this field, one receives in order to *give*, and it is this constant giving of oneself that makes the world of the professional a lonely one.

Mind you, being psychic does not enable you to change the course of history, but it will guide you into an acceptance of reality, or, as is often the case, it will show you how to cooperate with others in working to change some otherwise unchangeable tomorrows.

Many of the predictions mentioned in this book are *conditional;* many of them can be *avoided*. They may become reality *if* the deterioration of human society continues at its present pace. It is this "if" that sustains hope.

I cannot imagine a Higher Power wanting tragedy to befall the human race. God is unchangeable but also merciful, and with the channel open for impressions of guidance and love, nothing is impossible.

Learn how to change, and you can change others.

Learn how to love, and you can change the course of history!